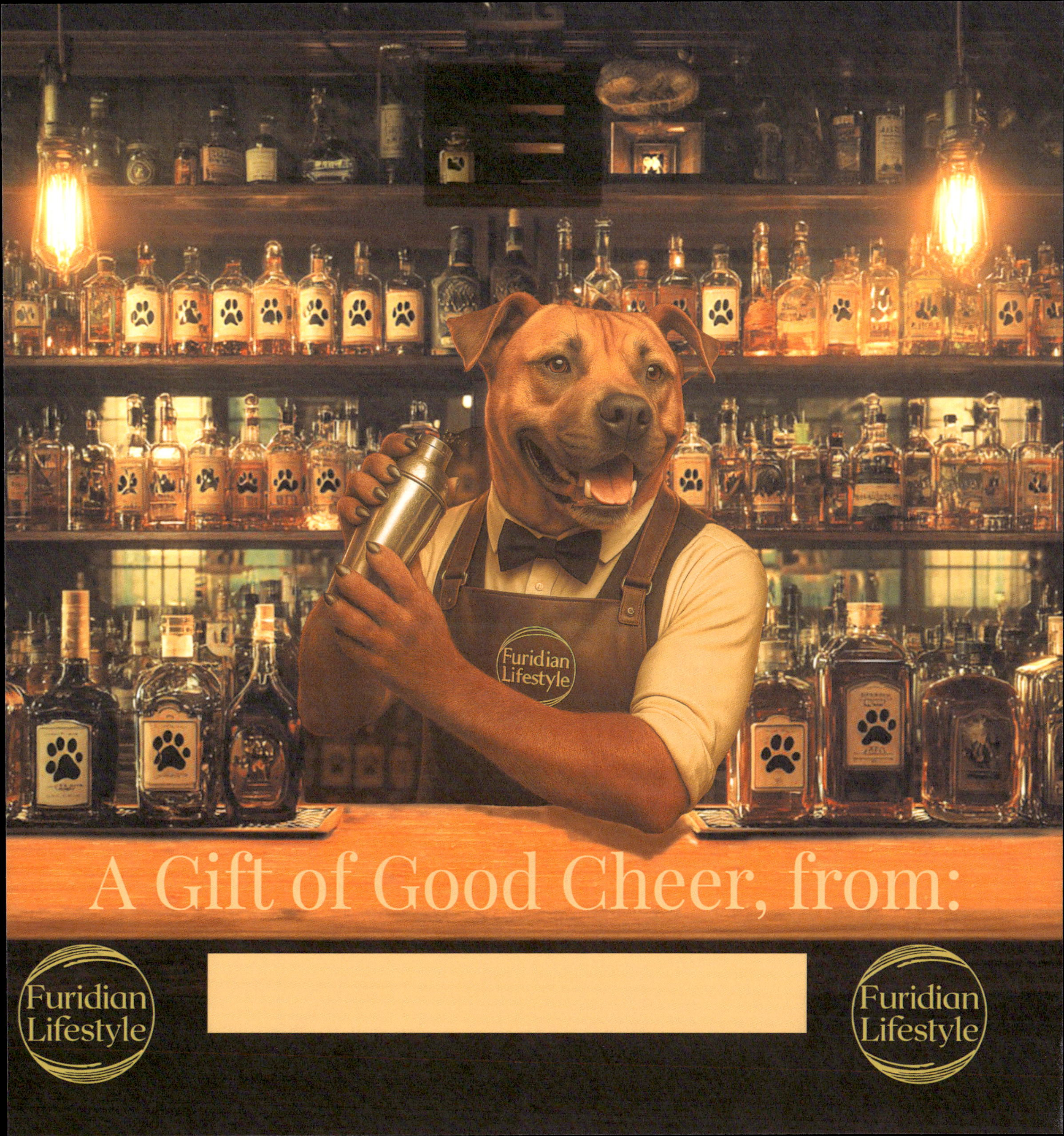
Furidian Lifestyle
A Gift of Good Cheer, from:
Furidian Lifestyle
Furidian Lifestyle

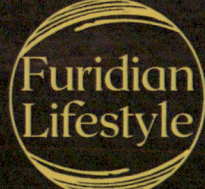

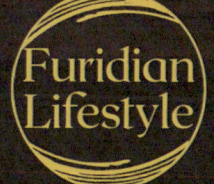

Furidian's Pawtender's Pour
A Lifestyle Guide to Dog-Safe Mocktails, Human Cocktails, Spirit History,
and the Rituals of Companionship.

Copyright © 2025 Furidian Lifestyle. All rights reserved.

No part of this publication may be reproduced, stored in a retrieval system,
or transmitted in any form or by any means - electronic, mechanical,
photocopying, recording, or otherwise without prior written permission of the publisher.

Published by Furidian Lifestyle
Fort Lauderdale, Florida

www.furidianlifestyle.com

ISBN: 979-8-218-78507-9 (Hardcover)
ISBN: 979-8-218-78508-6 (Softcover)

Printed in the United States of America

A portion of all proceeds supports "Furidian Friends,"
a nonprofit dedicated to rescuing and rehabilitating at-risk dogs.

Furidian's Pawtender's Pour

To the reader with a raised glass and a loyal friend nearby. This book found its way to you for a reason. Whether you've followed Furidian from the beginning or just joined the journey, know this: every page was made with heart, for the kind of people who believe dogs belong at happy hour and that the best moments are meant to be shared.

The Furidian Lifestyle is not for everyone; it requires intention, loyalty, and integrity.

This isn't just a drink recipe book. Inside, you'll find the history of spirits, the tools of the craft, and the standards behind every pour. You'll learn what is safe for your dog, what is not, and why it matters.

Nothing here is careless
The ingredients are clean
The glassware is proper
The ritual is earned

There are cocktails for you. Pawtails for your dog.

But this is not about the drinks. This book honors the bond between us, not with trends or tricks, but with knowledge, precision, and respect.

If you're chasing trends, look elsewhere.
If you're here to raise your standard and learn, you've got the right pawtender.

~ Furidian

Scan to Shop and Follow Furidian
FURIDIANLIFESTYLE.COM
Furidian Lifestyle™

Pawtails-Planners-Premium Products-
Pup Portraits and Prints-Pawsitive Rescue Stories

Welcome to the Bar
Furidian's story ~ A Tail Best Sipped Slowly

I was barely two weeks old when he found me, abandoned in a Florida dumpster, my paw mangled, my breath shallow, but my will intact. He called me Achilles, not for how I was wounded, but for how I endured when others would have given up. As he nursed me back to health, I learned loyalty, and we learned that some bonds transcend the ordinary tie between human and dog.

I wasn't born into luxury, but I rose toward it through deliberate, intentional choices and earned respect. What began as survival became something greater: a presence, a purpose, a legacy built on the understanding that true character isn't inherited, it's forged through adversity.

Achilles was the name I was given; Furidian is the name I chose to live up to. Furidian represents more than a name; it's a standard for how to carry yourself when no one's watching and how to lead when no one's following. This philosophy wasn't built from pedigree, but from the kind of character that stays loyal without condition, remains composed under pressure, protects what matters, and leads with both kindness and backbone.

Every scar became wisdom, every setback became a foundation for something stronger. I learned that the most meaningful luxury isn't what you're given, it's what you build when you refuse to settle for less than you're capable of becoming.

Now I lead not by barking orders, but by walking with purpose alongside those who understand that the best journeys, like the best drinks, are always meant to be shared.

~ Furidian

Furidian didn't inherit the lifestyle, he earned it.
And now he stands as proof that where you start doesn't define where you belong.

A portion of every purchase supports

Furidian Friends

our nonprofit dedicated to rescuing, rehabilitating, and rehoming at risk dogs. Turning discarded lives into legacies.

Ten Tenets of the Furidian Lifestyle (1-5)

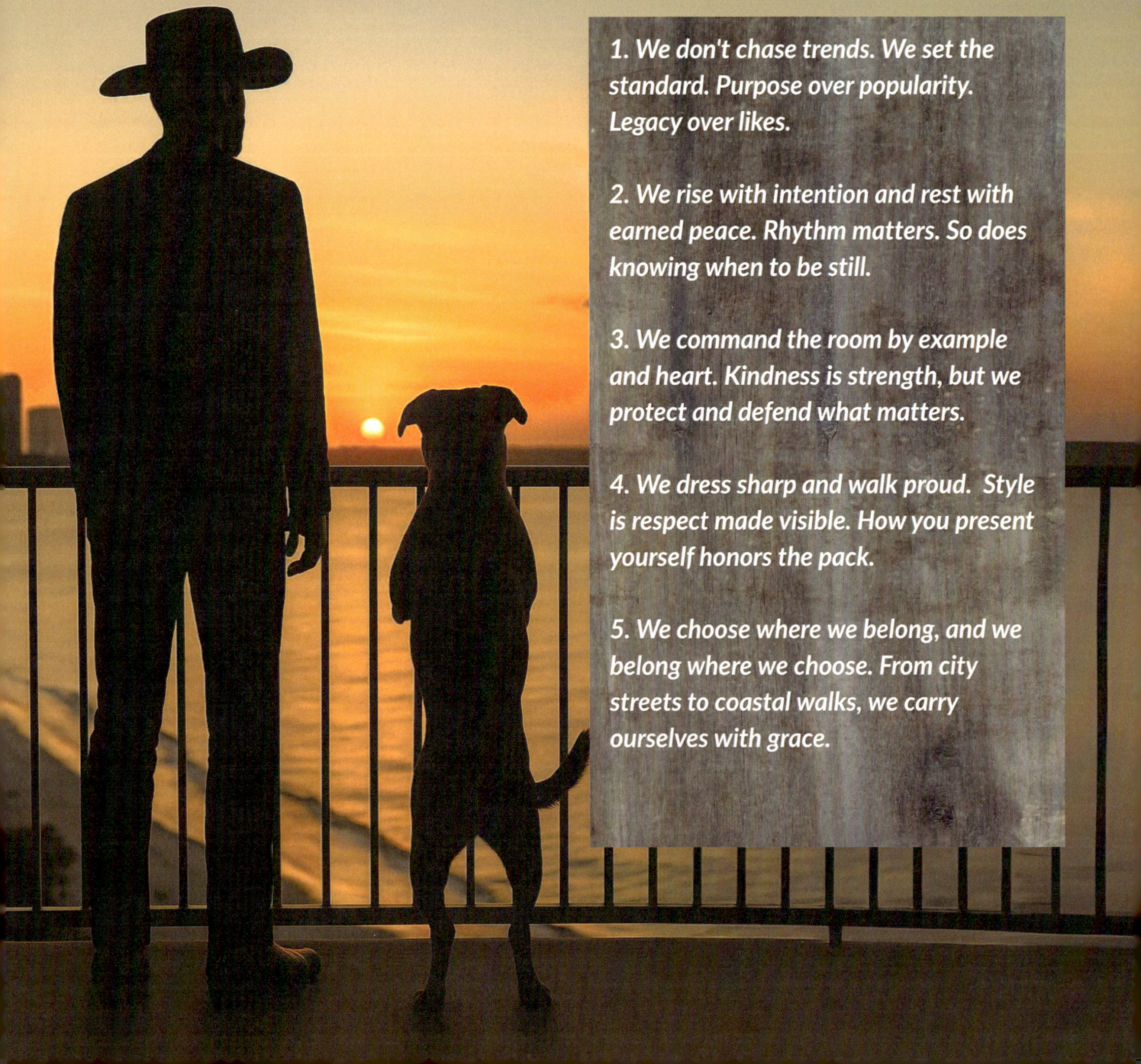

1. We don't chase trends. We set the standard. Purpose over popularity. Legacy over likes.

2. We rise with intention and rest with earned peace. Rhythm matters. So does knowing when to be still.

3. We command the room by example and heart. Kindness is strength, but we protect and defend what matters.

4. We dress sharp and walk proud. Style is respect made visible. How you present yourself honors the pack.

5. We choose where we belong, and we belong where we choose. From city streets to coastal walks, we carry ourselves with grace.

Ten Tenets of the Furidian Lifestyle (6-10)

6. We are not pets. We are partners. We walk beside, never behind. Loyalty flows both ways or it means nothing.

7. We don't ask for what we've already earned. Our presence is enough. Confidence needs no permission.

8. We live with impeccable taste and lead with unshakeable heart. Every detail matters, from the pour to the collar. Excellence is our baseline, not our ceiling.

9. Our character defines worth, not pedigree. Papers don't prove identity, and beginnings don't determine destiny.

10. We transform our scars, battles, and hard-earned lessons into our strength. Where we started was just the prologue. Now we write the story worth following.

🐾 *Furidian's Pawtender's Quick Start Guide*

For those who infuse everyday rituals with taste, meaning, and companionship

*Furidian's Pawtender's Pour isn't just a recipe book,
it's a celebration of ritual, connection,
and the shared joy between human and hound.*

savor the pour,
cherish the company

For the Human

- Each human recipe is a crafted cocktail or mocktail
- Suggested glassware, garnishes, and optional spirits elevate presentation
- Use fresh ingredients, clean ice, and pour slowly
- Savor the ritual, never rush

For the Dog

- The paw icon next to the Pawtail Title indicates recipes for your dog.
- **When in doubt, check with your vet before introducing anything new**
- All dog-friendly pours use vet-reviewed, safe ingredients designed to hydrate, nourish, or simply bond
- *Start small, if unsure, choose the smaller portion*
- *Serve cool, never iced. Cold can upset sensitive stomachs*
- *Use a clean bowl or pup-safe glass*
- *Garnishes are optional*
- **Always monitor** your dog for their first sip, and allow a quick sniff test before serving
- These drinks are **occasional treats** to celebrate, not replacements for water or meals

Paw = Dog Recipe

Furidian Lifestyle; It's not about mixing drinks, it's about mixing meaning into the moment.

Pawtender's Party Guide
How to host a pet-friendly cocktail night

Furidian's Party Pour Philosophy

Good Company
Better Cocktails
Best Friends

> Never pour before the paws arrive. Always greet your guests, two-legged and four, with a handshake, a pat, and a refreshment.

- Send formal invites... to the humans
  The dogs already know
- Chill your dog-safe mixers
  (goat milk, broth, purees)
- Freeze fancy ice molds - paws, bones, or yogurt cubes for flair
- Stock the "Bark Bar" with labeled jars
  Keep it classy. Keep it clear
- Set a no-chocolate, no-xylitol zone
  Strictly enforced - No exceptions
- Place water bowls at all levels
  Not just floor-level
- Space out snack zones
  Avoid crowding and food side-eye
- Create cozy lounging areas
  Grass mats, cushions, or a fleece zone
- Offer both leashed & leash-free zones
  Match energy levels, not just fur types

Drink Pairings
Match every human cocktail with a pawtail alternative
Serve dogs first, it keeps them calm while you pour

RULE 1

This is a cocktail affair, not a campsite. Break out the dog-safe glass or polished steel for your four-legged guests. **Respect the pour.**

Furidian's Pawtender's Pantry

*Before you shake that shaker or pour that broth, clear the bar top.
Not everything that looks tasty belongs in your dog's bowl.*

This curated list from Furidian separates the safe sips from the toxic trips, so you can mix with confidence and intention.

Each serving is designed as a **supplemental treat —never a meal**. Adjust for your dog's age, weight, activity level, and body condition.

Every recipe in this book was crafted using guidance from trusted veterinary sources including: ASPCA Animal Poison Control, AKC Canine Nutrition, and the Pet Poison Helpline (VCA Network).

⚠ **Always consult your vet before introducing new ingredients, even vet-approved ones may not suit every pup**

Furidian's Pawma's Promise:
Only the safest sips and tail-wagging toppers

VETERINARY PRESCRIPTION

Pawma Furidian's Golden Rule
"One pour a day keeps the vet bills away."
🦴 Pour with intention
🦴 Use vet-approved ingredients only
🦴 Serve in peace, love, and pawtection

Pawma Furidian

TOXIC - Off the doggie Menu
These ingredients are strictly banned!

Hard "No" List
DO NOT SERVE

- Xylitol — Deadly sweetener in PB, some chocolate, & drinks
- Chocolate / Cocoa — Toxic theobromine affects heart & nerves
- Grapes — Can cause acute kidney failure
- Raisins — Can cause acute kidney failure
- Caffeine — Causes seizures, hyperactivity
- Alcohol — Even small sips = big problems
- Macadamia Nuts — Linked to tremors, vomiting
- Nutmeg — Causes hallucinations and toxicity
- Artificial Sweeteners — Erythritol, sorbitol = upset or toxic
- Onions — Damages red blood cells
- Garlic — Damages red blood cells
- Chives — Damages red blood cells
- Cherry Pits — Contain cyanide + choking hazard
- Raw Dough / Yeast — Expands in stomach, alcohol byproduct
- Fatty Scraps / Butter — Triggers pancreatitis
- Moldy Foods — Can contain tremor-inducing toxins

ASPCA Poison Control
1-800-426-4435

Just like any great bartender, the best ones know what to keep off the menu.

Serve smart.
Shake responsibly.

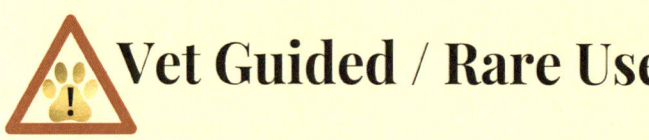
⚠ Vet Guided / Rare Use

 Ceylon Cinnamon — Tiny pinch only; NEVER Cassia

 Fresh Ginger — Small amounts; spicy to some dogs

 Milk — Most dogs are lactose intolerant

 Cheese — Most dogs are lactose intolerant

 Ice Cream — Most dogs are lactose intolerant. Some flavors like chocolate or sugar-free varieties may contain zylitol, which is toxic.

Just because you can eat it, doesn't mean they should. Be the bartender your dog thinks you are, classy, informed, and always watching the bowl!

 Citrus (lemon, lime, orange, grapefruit) — Juice can cause upset stomach

 Tomatoes (unripe) — Contain solanine when green

 Bread (white, processed) — Filler food, no benefit

 Salt / Salty Foods — Excess = sodium poisoning

 Nuts (general) — High fat, choking risk, often salted

Furidian's Approved Bark Back List
A bartender-style breakdown of safe ingredients for your pet's pawtail

House Fruits & Muddled Additions
Fresh, seasonal, and <u>always seedless</u>

 Blueberries — Antioxidants for that radiant coat glow

 Bananas — Natural sweetness + potassium hit

 Apples (no seeds) — Classic crunch, digestion support

 Strawberries — Natural sweetness + Vitamin C

 Watermelon (no rind/seeds) — Refreshing, hydrating

 Mango (no pit) — Silky, vitamin-rich

 Pineapple (no core) — Aids digestion in small bites

Pears (no seeds) — Sweet, fiber-rich

Mixers & Bases

 Water, filtered always best

 Coconut water

 Low-Sodium Bone Broth

 *Goat's Milk (lactose-free)*

 Plain Goat Yogurt (lactose-free)

The Garden Pour Portfolio
Garden-to-Bowl Freshness, Bark-Tender Approved

Furidian Seeds
- Cucumber
- Carrots
- Green Beans
- Pumpkin
- Spinach
- Parsley
- Mint
- Sweet Potato

Flavor Enhancers
- Peanut Butter *(xylitol-free only)*
- Rolled Oats *(cooked or soaked)*
- Raw Honey *(tiny amount, dogs over 1 year old)*
- Fresh Ginger *(pinch only)*
- Ceylon Cinnamon *(never Cassia)*
- Carob Powder *(chocolatey & dog-safe)*

Furidian's Approved Garnish and Splashes
Wholesome garnishes to elevate hydration, digestion, and indulgence

Golden Glow Broth
Soothing, savory, and sippable, perfect for comfort and hydration

Ingredients:
- 1 oz Unsalted chicken bone broth
- ½ oz Carrot juice
- ¼ oz Apple water or juice
- Drop of lemon peel oil (use zest, <u>not juice</u>) for aroma

Watermelon Rosettes
Elegant, hydrating garnish for summer pawtails

Ingredients:
- Seedless watermelon
- Optional: mint leaf or basil sliver for visual accent

Instructions:
- Use a thin slicer or melon baller to form small rosette shapes or simple spheres
- Chill before serving for maximum refreshment

Frozen Yogurt Treats
Cool, creamy relief for sun-soaked afternoons

Ingredients:
- 1 cup Plain yogurt
- ½ cup Diced fruit

Instructions:
- Mix ingredients, pour into bone or pawprint molds, freeze, and serve chilled

Storage:
- Keep in the freezer for up to 3 months
- Serve directly from the freezer for a cool, crisp treat

Carrot-Coconut Crunchers
Tropical texture treats to balance sweet pawtails

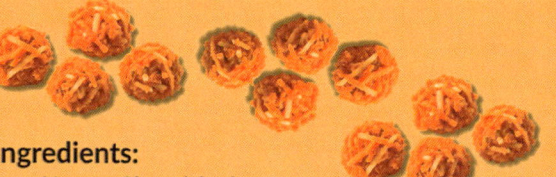

Ingredients:
- ½ cup Shredded carrot
- ¼ cup Unsweetened shredded coconut
- 1 tbsp Flaxseed meal (optional binder)
- Splash of carrot or pineapple juice

Instructions:
- Mix all ingredients into bite-sized clumps
- Shape
- Dehydrate (or bake at low temp until crisp)

Every garnish here is pup-approved, but always start small to suit your dog's taste and tummy.

🐾 Furidian's Approved Whipped Pup Cup
Add a pup cloud to your doggie drinks for extra flavor fun!

Whipped Cloud Cream
Fluffy, Dairy-Free Coconut Topping for Paw-sitive Moments

Ingredients:
- 1 can full-fat coconut cream (chilled 24-48 hrs)
- Optional: 1 tsp raw honey (dogs over 1 yr)

Equipment:
- Hand or stand mixer
- Large chilled mixing bowl
- Chilled beaters

Instructions:
1. Freeze bowl and beaters for 10 mins.
2. Scoop only solid cream into bowl (no liquid).
3. Add honey if desired (for dogs over 1 yr).
4. Whip on high for 1-2 mins until peaks form.
5. Serve immediately or refrigerate to firm.

Storage: Store in airtight container up to 5 days. Re-whip if needed.

Furidian Tip: Pipe onto chilled fruit, freeze into bites, or top a mocktail.

Ditch the Can. Go Clean.

- Most store-bought whipped creams are loaded with dairy, sugar, gums, and preservatives your dog doesn't need.
- Ours is different: light, natural, and crafted with just a few vet-approved ingredients for pure, pup-safe indulgence.

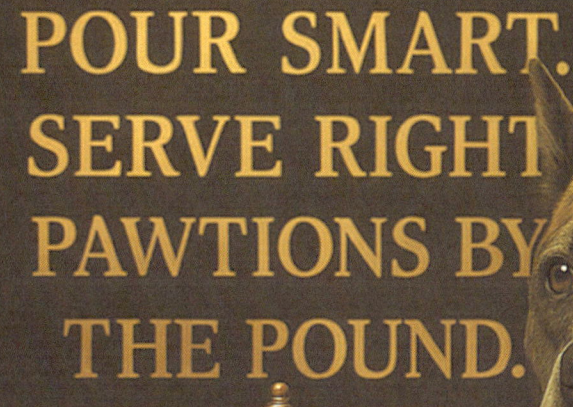

Pour Smart. Serve Right. Portion by the Pound
What Does "Pour" Mean in This Book.

🐾 In The Pawtender's Pour, "pour" refers to the total liquid volume of a single serving of a dog-friendly pawtail recipe, measured in fluid ounces. Each pour is carefully portioned to match your dog's weight range, using guidelines informed by veterinary nutritionists.

When we say "Pour 1–2 ounces", we mean:
- 1–2 fluid ounces (30–60 mL) of total liquid
- This is a measured pour, not an open-ended free pour.

Designed to be a supplemental treat, not a meal replacement. This allows your dog to enjoy flavor, hydration, and enrichment without disrupting their daily caloric balance.

Always consult your vet before introducing new treats.

Pours are intentional, measured, and tailored by weight class.
Pour with Intention. Serve with Confidence.

The Pawfect Pour Chart
Match your dog's weight to their pour
One pour is paw-lenty on spacial occasions

Even safe ingredients can affect breeds differently. Start small and monitor your pup.

SAFE SERVING SIZE

Weight	Oz	mL	Tbs	Tsp
Under 5 lbs	0.5–1	15–30	1–2	3–6
5–10 lbs	1–2	30–60	2–4	6–12
11–25 lbs	2–3	60–90	4–6	12–18
26–50 lbs	3–5	90–150	6–10	18–30
51–75 lbs	5–7	150–210	10–14	30–42
Over 75 lbs	7–9	210–270	14–18	42–54

Pour Smart. Serve Right. Portion by the Pound.

Sip-Worthy Sizes for Mighty Minis.

Under 10 Pounds
Pour 1-2 ounces

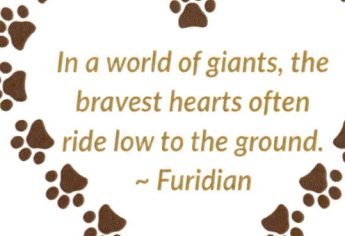

In a world of giants, the bravest hearts often ride low to the ground.
~ Furidian

Toy Poodle · Brussels Griffon · Biewer Terrier · Chinese Crested Dog · Japanese Chin · Toy Fox Terrier

Affenpinscher · Chihuahua · Yorkshire Terrier · Maltese · Papillon · Pomeranian

Pour Smart. Serve Right. Portion by the Pound.
Fetch with Purpose. Love with Loyalty.

50-75 Pounds
Pour 5-7 ounces

Basset Hound · Portuguese Water Dog · Standard Poodle · Golden Retriever · Labrador Retriever · Chesapeake Bay Retriever · German Shorthaired Pointer

Every pour honors the friend always by your side

Pour Smart. Serve Right. Portion by the Pound.
Giants Among Dogs. Gentle at the Core.

Over 75 Pounds
Pour 7-9 ounces

Irish Wolfhound
32-35 inches
105-180 pounds

Great Dane
30-34 inches
110-175 pounds

English Mastiff
27-32 inches
120-230 pounds

Black Russian Terrier
27-30 inches
80-130 pounds

Anatolian Shepherd
27-29 inches
90-150 pounds

Saint Bernard
26-30 inches
120-180 pounds

Newfoundland
26-28 inches
100-150 pounds

Doberman Pinscher
24-28 inches
75-100 pounds

Pour Smart. Serve Right. Portion by the Pound.
Built for Strength. Born for Bond.

Over 75 Pounds
Pour 7-9 ounces

A true Furidian doesn't bark to be heard, he stands, and the room listens. ~ Furidian

Cane Corso
24-27 inches
90-120 pounds

Beuceron
24-27 inches
70-110 pounds

German Shepherd
24-26 inches
75-100 pounds

Alaskan Malamute
23-25 inches
75-85 pounds

Bernese Mountain Dog
23-27 inches
80-115 pounds

Rottweiler
23-27 inches
90-135 pounds

Old English Sheep Dog
22-24 inches
70-100 pounds

American bulldog
22-25 inches
75-100 pounds

Furidian Pawtender's Favorite Recipes
Information worth repeating!

For the Human
- Each human recipe is a crafted cocktail or mocktail
- Suggested glassware, garnishes, and optional spirits elevate presentation
- Use fresh ingredients, clean ice, and pour slowly
- Savor the ritual, never rush

 **Check ID- NEVER Serve Alcohol to Minors (under 21 in USA)**

 **Do NOT serve Alcohol to dogs!**

For the Dog
- The <u>paw icon</u> next to the Pawtail Title indicates recipes for your dog.
- **When in doubt, <u>check with your vet</u> before introducing anything new**
- All dog-friendly pours use vet-reviewed, safe ingredients designed to hydrate, nourish, or simply bond
- Start small, if unsure, choose the smaller portion
- <u>**Always monitor**</u> your dog for their first sip, and allow a quick sniff test before serving

ASPCA Poison Control 1-800-426-4435

The Signature Furidian Martini

*A vodka should be clean, not soulless.
If it burns, it's cheap.
If it vanishes, it's water.
The sweet spot is clarity with character.
~ Furidian*

Martini

Ingredients:
2 ½ oz Vodka or Gin

Style:
- **Perfect:** ¼ oz Dry vermouth, ¼ oz sweet vermouth
- **Regular:** ¼ oz dry vermouth
- **Dry:** 2-3 Drops dry vermouth
- **Extra Dry:** No vermouth
- **Dirty:** ¼ oz Olive juice, olive garnish
- **Gibson:** Garnished with pickled onion
- **Vesper:** Shaken, not stirred, James Bond's custom mix of Gin, Vodka, and Lillet Blanc

Glassware:
- **Martini glass:** Straight up
- **Rocks glass:** On the Rocks

Instructions: Add all ingredients to a shaker with ice
- **Shaken:** Shake until icy cold. Strain into a chilled glass
- **Stirred:** Stir and strain into a chilled glass

Garnish: Lemon Twist or 3-6 stuffed green olives (regular or blue cheese)

Mission
Sip. Shake. Stay.

🐾 Bark, James Bark

Ingredients:
- 2 oz Unsalted chicken bone broth
- 1 tsp Finely chopped green olive (rinsed, no brine or pit)
- Splash of cucumber water

Glassware: Mini stainless steel pup shot bowl

Garnish: Carrot stick. Tiny pinch of parsley (optional garnish)

Espresso Martini

Espresso Martini

Ingredients:
2 oz Vodka
1 oz Coffee Liqueor
1 oz Freshly brewed hot Espresso
Optional: Simple syrup for sweetness

Glassware:
- Martini or Coupe glass

Instructions:
- Brew a fresh espresso shot - this is crucial for a rich crema
- Add vodka, coffee liqueur, espresso, and simple syrup to a cocktail shaker filled with ice
- Shake vigorously for 15–20 seconds

    The hot espresso hitting the cold ice creates that signature frothy top

- Strain into a chilled coupe or martini glass

Garnish: Float three coffee beans on the foam

Furidian's Pro Tip: For a luxurious twist, try substituting vanilla vodka or adding a dash of chocolate bitters. If you want a creamy version, add ½ oz Baileys or a splash of cold brew concentrate for more coffee depth.

They say three beans bring health, wealth, and happiness, but I believe they stand for heart, hustle, and hope. The first wakes you up, the second keeps you moving, and the third reminds you why it's worth it.
~ Furidian

🐾 *Pupresso Martini*

Ingredients:
- 2 oz unsalted beef or chicken bone broth (cooled)
- 1 oz unsweetened coconut milk or goat's milk
- ½ tsp carob powder (a safe, caffeine-free chocolate substitute)
- Ice (optional, for chill)

Instructions:
- Shake and Serve

Glassware: Mini stainless steel pup shot bowl

Garnish: 3 roasted chickpeas, or 3 small carob chips (to echo the coffee beans)

Classic, Straight Up or On the Rocks

The Manhattan

The Manhattan didn't ask to be famous, it simply entered the room, well-dressed, and let the world adjust.

Some say the Manhattan was first poured at the Manhattan Club in the 1870s, during a political affair hosted for Lady Randolph Churchill. The story has flair, but as with many cocktails, elegance often outruns accuracy.

Then there's the Broadway bartender known only as Black, who stirred the first Manhattan in the 1860s near Houston Street. Years later, fellow barkeep William F. Mulhall of the Hoffman House vouched for this tale. And when one legend confirms another, you learn to lean in.

The earliest written proof? 1882, Olean, New York. A small note in the paper spoke of a new favorite: whiskey, vermouth, bitters, called the Manhattan. A quiet mention, yet it spoke volumes, just like the pour.

The Manhattan

Ingredients:
- 2 oz Bourbon
- 1 ounce Sweet Vermouth
- 2 Dashes Angostura Bitters

Instructions:
Add all ingredients to a shaker with ice.
Shake or Stir until icy cold
Strain into a **coupe** or a **rocks** glass

Garnish: Cherry or Lemon Twist

🐾 Barkhattan

Never shaken. Always stirred with care, class, and canine wellness in mind.

Ingredients:
- 1 oz Unsweetened beet juice
- 1 oz Low-sodium bone broth (beef or chicken)
- ½ tsp Pure apple cider vinegar
- 1 drop Dog-safe vanilla alcohol-free, glycerin-based only extract (optional)
- Ice cubes made from frozen broth or water

Old Fashioned

In the early 1800s, a *"cocktail"* was defined as spirits, sugar, water, and bitters. That's it.

As bartenders got fancy with muddled fruits and liqueurs, traditionalists pushed back, asking for a drink made "the old-fashioned way." And thus, the name was born.

When the world got fancy, one drink stayed loyal to the basics. The Old Fashioned

Old Fashioned

Rocks

Old Fashioned

Ingredients:
- 2 oz Bourbon or Rye
- 1 Sugar cube (or ½ tsp simple syrup)
- 2–3 dashes Angostura bitters
- Splash of water

Glassware: Old Fashioned or Rocks Glass

Instructions:
- Place the sugar cube in the glass
- Add bitters and a small splash of water
- Muddle until dissolved
- Add bourbon and stir gently
- Express orange peel over the drink and drop it into the glass

Garnish: Large clear ice cube, Orange Peel. Optional: Luxardo cherry

🐾 Bow-Wow Old Fashioned

Ingredients:
- ¼ cup Beef or chicken bone broth (unsalted, pet-safe)
- 1–2 tbsp Unsweetened apple juice (optional for sweetness)
- Crushed ice or a large frozen goat milk cube

Instructions:
- Combine broth and juice in a mixing cup
- Pour over a frozen goat milk cube or crushed ice in a pup-safe glass
- Garnish 1 small dog biscuit or freeze-dried meat stick. Optional: thin apple slice for extra flair

PawMa Furidian's Favorite – Margarita

Margarita

Ingredients:
- 2 oz Tequila
- 1 oz Orange liqueur
- 1 oz Fresh lime juice
- ½–¾ oz Agave syrup (adjust to taste)
- Flaky sea salt + Tajín (for rim)

Instructions: On the Rocks
- Rim a chilled rocks glass generously with sea salt and Tajín
- In a shaker, combine tequila, orange liqueur, lime juice, and agave
- Shake well with ice and strain over fresh ice into the rimmed glass
- Optional: Add a splash of soda water for lift

Instructions: Frozen/Blended
- Rim a wide margarita glass with a mix of salt and lime zest
- Blend tequila, orange liqueur, lime juice, agave, and 1 cup of ice until slushy
- Pour into the prepared glass and serve immediately
- Optional: Add a splash of orange juice for extra smoothness

Garnish: Lime wedge or dehydrated lime wheel

DID YOU KNOW? The word 'margarita' means daisy in Spanish. It's thought to be a twist on a classic Daisy cocktail: citrus, sweetener, and spirit over ice.

🐾 The Barkarita Blanca

Ingredients:
- ¼ cup Coconut water (no added sugar)
- 2 tbsp Cucumber purée (or finely strained juice)
- Tiny bit of Lime peel (zest, <u>not juice</u>)
- Tiny pinch of pet-safe sodium-free broth powder (optional for "salt" vibe)
- Crushed ice
- Shredded coconut or finely crushed freeze-dried chicken treat for "rim"

Directions:
- Lightly moisten the rim of a shallow pup-safe bowl with water
- Press into coconut or chicken treat dust to mimic a salted rim
- Blend coconut water, cucumber purée, lime peel zest, and broth powder
- Pour over crushed ice in the rimmed bowl.
- Serve chilled, with supervision and tail wags

Some PawMas knit…
I host happy hour with Pawtails and love served chilled.
~ Furidian's Pawma

Furidian's Bloody Best

Bloody Mary

Ingredients:
- 2 oz Vodka
- 4 oz Tomato juice
- ½ oz Fresh lemon juice
- 2 dashes Worcestershire sauce
- 2 dashes Hot sauce
- 1 pinch Celery salt
- 1 pinch Ground black pepper

Instructions:
- Rim a tall glass with celery salt (optional)
- Fill glass with ice
- In a shaker, combine all liquid ingredients and seasonings
- Shake lightly
- Pour into the glass

Garnish Screwer: Typical: celery stalk, olives, pickle spear, lemon wedge - but get creative and load up your garnish skewer like you're building a skyline

🐾 The Hair of the Dog

Ingredients:
- ½ cup Low-sodium beef bone broth (cooled)
- ¼ cup Puréed cooked carrots
- 1 tbsp Diluted unsweetened tomato purée **(no salt/onions/garlic)**
- 1 tsp Finely chopped celery
- 1 Dog treat or biscuit "garnish" (optional)
- Shredded coconut or finely crushed freeze-dried chicken treat for "rim"

Directions:
- Blend bone broth, carrots, tomato purée, and celery until smooth
- Serve chilled in a stainless-steel bowl
- Top with a biscuit for flair

Jello Shots

Classic Jello Shots

Ingredients:
- 1 cup boiling water
- 1 box flavored Jell-O (3 oz, pick your flavor: strawberry, lime, etc.)
- ½ cup cold water
- ½ cup vodka (or rum, tequila, flavored spirits)

Use flavored vodka (like vanilla, citron, or whipped cream) to match the Jell-O for dessert-style shots.

Instructions:
- In a bowl or large measuring cup, whisk 1 cup boiling water into the Jell-O powder until completely dissolved (about 2 minutes)
- Stir in ½ cup cold water and ½ cup vodka
- Pour into 1–2 oz plastic shot cups or silicone molds
- Refrigerate for 3–4 hours or until fully set
- Serve cold.
- Optional: Garnish with whipped cream sugar rims, or fruit bits

---

Wag-worthy wobble in every cube

 Wobble Wag

Ingredients:
- 1 cup unsalted chicken or beef bone broth (cooled, no onion or garlic)
- 2 tbsp blueberry purée (or finely mashed fresh blueberries)
- 1 tbsp plain, unflavored gelatin - **Do NOT** use Jell-O it contains xylitol
- Optional: Pinch of Ceylon Cinamon or Carob Powder

Instructions:
- In a small saucepan, warm ½ cup of the broth over low heat—**do not boil**
- Sprinkle in the gelatin slowly while whisking. Stir until fully dissolved (1–2 min)
- Remove from heat. Add the remaining ½ cup of broth and blueberry purée
- Mix well
- Pour into silicone dog themed molds, ice cube trays, or a shallow glass dish
- Chill in the refrigerator for at least 3–4 hours until fully set
- Pop out and store in an airtight container in the fridge for up to 5 days

Furidian Tip:
Use bone broth + beet juice for a vibrant red pawtail cube
Serve as a floating *"ice chip"* in a *Pup Cup* or a chewy topper for meals

⚠ AVOID

Flavored gelatin (like Jell-O): often contains xylitol, added sugars, artificial dyes, and preservatives.

Xylitol or other artificial sweeteners: extremely **TOXIC** to dogs, even in small amounts.

Shooters and Puppy Slurpers

SHOOTER	 SLURPER
 **Lemon Drop** 1½ oz Citron Vodka Splash of Sour or Lemon Juice Sugar Lemon	**Lemon Lick** Bone Broth Lemon Ice Chip Pup Cloud Parsley Dust
 **B-52 (Layer)** ½ oz Kahlua ½ oz Baileys ½ oz Grand Mariner Whip Cream	**B-Furty-Two** Goat Milk, Carob Swirl Pup Cloud
 **Purple Hooter** 1 oz Vodka 1 oz Chambord 1 oz Lime Juice ¼ Simple Syrup	**Purple Velvet** Blueberry Beet Glow Broth
 **Washington Apple** 1 oz Crown Royal 1 oz Apple Schnapps Splash Cranberry	**Crisp Collar** Apple Juice Beet Splash Cranberry
 **Chocolate Cake** 1 oz Frangelico 1 oz Citron Vodka Sugared Lemon	**Toast of the Town** Goat Milk ¼ tsp Carob Powder ¼ tsp Nutritional Yeast (adds cake-like richness) Pup Cloud
 **Cinnamon Toast Crunch** 1 oz Fireball ½ oz Rumchata Cinnamon Rim	**Cinna-Sniff Crunch** 1 oz Goat Milk ¼ tsp Ceylon Cinnamon ¼ tsp carob Powder

Good Dogs

Great Drinks

Furidian Lifestyle

Arctic Intentions

Tail Wag Review:
- ☐ Licked clean
- ☐ Needed coaxing
- ☐ Turned up nose

Sharp winds, smooth pours, and paws made for snow.

Furidian's Winter Rule #1: Chill in the bowl. Warm in the heart.

Class never chills. Only the drinks do.

Arctic Ember

Ingredients:
- 1½ oz Vodka
- ½ oz Fresh lemon juice
- ½ oz White cranberry juice
- ¼ oz Lapsang souchong syrup or 1 drop Liquid smoke (optional)
- Top with sparkling water

Glassware: Chilled rocks glass

Garnish: Lemon twist + sprig of thyme

🐾 Snowpaw Spritz

Ingredients:
- ¼ cup Cold coconut water
- 1 tbsp Unsweetened pear purée
- Tiny bit of Lemon peel (zest, not juice)
- Optional: Frozen into snowflake molds

Garnish: Tiny ice cube with edible flower petals. Use rose petals or calendula for a white/yellow January vibe. **(Organic and pesticide-free!)**

Love Unleashed or Pour Decisions

Where chocolate melts and diamonds shine, love lives.

Tail Wag Review:
- ☐ Licked clean
- ☐ Needed coaxing
- ☐ Turned up nose

"Tonight's special: velvet pours, heart-shaped snacks, and love that doesn't leave after dessert."
~Furidian

Furidian's Real Love Rule #1:
If they don't share snacks or sofa space, it's not love

Velvet Valentine

Ingredients:
- 1½ oz Vodka
- 1 oz Chocolate liquor
- ½ oz Raspberry liquor
- 1 oz Heavy cream or oat milk (for dairy-free luxe)

Glassware: Coupe or martini glass

Garnish: Shaved chocolate + fresh raspberry

🐾 Cupid's Crunch

Ingredients:
- ¼ cup Unsweetened coconut water (chilled)
- 1 tbsp Plain goat milk yogurt
- 1 tsp Finely diced strawberries (fresh, not mashed)
- ½ tsp Crushed freeze-dried apple chips (for crunch, NO SEEDS)
- Optional: Tiny heart-shaped freeze-dried treat on top

Instructions:
- Pour chilled coconut water into a shallow clear bowl
- Add a dollop of yogurt in the center (do not stir)
- Sprinkle diced strawberries and freeze-dried apple chips for visual pop and texture
- Top with a small heart treat for flair

Emerald Blood, Iron Heart

March with pride. Lead with purpose.

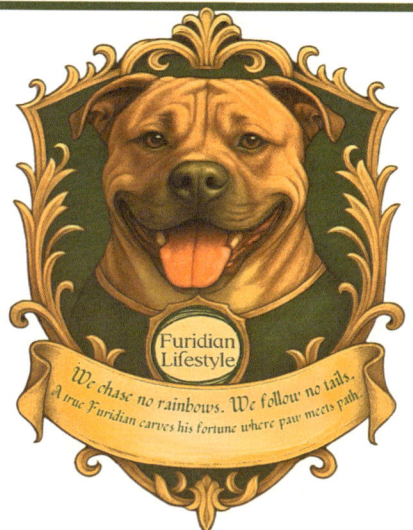

Furidian's Emerald Rule #1: The wind may test your coat, but never allow it to test your character

Emerald Giant

Ingredients:
- 2 oz Irish Whiskey
- ¾ oz Fresh lemon juice
- ½ oz Honey syrup
- ¼ oz Green chartreuse
- 1 Dash orange bitters

Glassware: Shake with ice and strain into a gold rimmed rocks glass over a large cube

Garnish: gold sugar rim + mint sprig

🐾 Shamrock Shake-up

Ingredients:
- ¼ cup Plain goat milk
- 1 tbsp Unsweetened cucumber purée (strained)
- ¼ tsp Chopped mint leaves (fresh, not extract)
- 1 tsp Plain goat yogurt
- Crushed ice
- Optional: Edible green spirulina powder (tiny pinch for color)

Instructions:
Stir all ingredients until smooth and serve over crushed ice in a shallow bowl. Top with a mint leaf or a frozen yogurt cube for garnish.

Tail Wag Review:
- ☐ Licked clean
- ☐ Needed coaxing
- ☐ Turned up nose

Puddles, Pipes, and Proper Pours

Furidian's April Showers Rule #1: Never trust a dry gentleman on a wet day.

A gentleman never splashes, unless he's serving.

Furidian's Puddle Jumper

Ingredients:
- 1½ oz Gin
- Fill with Elderflower tonic
- Splash of lemon
- Optional: Rain droplet served naturally

Glassware: Highball

Garnish: Cucumber ribbon & thyme sprig

🐾 Furidian's Drizzle

Ingredients:
- 2 oz cooled cucumber water
- 1 tsp Bone broth
- Pinch of mint or parsley (optional)

Tail Wag Review:
- ☐ Licked clean
- ☐ Needed coaxing
- ☐ Turned up nose

"A little weather never ruins a proper drink, just the wrong company." ~Furidian

Petals, Pours, and New Paws

🐾 *Strength knows softness. Power knows peace. When the sun warms the petals, remember kindness is the softest armor with the strongest hold. ~ Furidian*

Tail Wag Review:
- ☐ Licked clean
- ☐ Needed coaxing
- ☐ Turned up nose

Furidian's Spring Rule #1: Sip slow, Sniff flowers, Savor the breeze

Meadow Mojito

Ingredients:
- 2 oz Irish Whiskey
- ¾ oz Lemon juice
- ½ oz Honey syrup
- ¼ oz Green chartreuse
- 1 Dash orange bitters
- 6 Mint leaves

Glassware: Shake with ice, strain into coupe or vintage rocks glass

Garnish: sugar rim + mint + pressed edible flower

🐾 Mint Pup Float

Ingredients:
- ¼ cup Goat milk (plain)
- 1 tbsp Cucumber water
- ¼ tsp Chopped mint leaves
- 1 Goat milk frozen yogurt cube (flower-shaped)

Garnish: edible dog-safe flower petal or mint leaf

Furidian's Go Bag
- 💧 Water
- 🟫 Blanket
- ☂️ Umbrella
- 🥏 Frisbee
- 🦴 Snacks
- 🗑️ Waste bags
- 🧻 Paw wipes

Zest in Show: Brunch Club Edition

Furidian's Brunch Rule #1:
Lean in and spill the tea, not the cocktail

Summer Snap

Ingredients:
- 2 oz Citron Vodka
- ½ oz Cointreau or triple sec
- **Splash:** Sprite and sour

Glassware: Shake with ice and strain into a sugar-rimmed martini glass

Garnish: Lemon twist

🐾 Lemon Lick Drop

Ingredients:
- ¼ cup Chamomile tea, cold (caffeine-free, unsweetened)
- 1 tbsp Plain goat milk yogurt
- Tiny bit of Lemon peel oil, (use zest, *not juice*)
- ½ tsp honey (only for dogs over 1 year)
- 1–2 thin slices cucumber (optional for light freshness)

Instructions:
Whisk Ingredients
Serve over crushed ice in a chilled bowl

Garnish: Cucumber twist or frozen honey cube for flair

Tail Wag Review:
- ☐ Licked clean
- ☐ Needed coaxing
- ☐ Turned up nose

Stars and Stripes

To the guardians of our freedom and our independence, two-legged and four, we raise this glass in your honor.

Furidian Freedom: Red, White, and Blue Layered Cocktail

Furidian's Firework Rule #1: Protect those ears!

Ingredients:
- 🔴 (Bottom) 1 oz Grenadine
- ⚪ (Middle) 1 oz White Rum or Vodka (Lemonade/Coconut water for non-alcoholic)
- 🔵 Blue Layer (Top) 1 oz Blue Curaçao (or blue raspberry lemonade for non-alcoholic)
- Splash of sparkling water for fizz
- 🧊 Use slow-melt crushed ice or large cubes to help layers stay separated

Glassware: Highball

Garnish:
Mini skewer with blueberries, strawberries, and a white marshmallow
US Mini flag pick or firework straw

Instructions: (Layering)
- Add grenadine first.
- Fill highball glass slowly with ice to the top.
- Pour Rum, Vodka, or coconut water/lemonade gently over the back of a spoon to float.
- Top with blue curaçao or blue lemonade the same way.
- Finish with garnish.

🐾 Pawtriotic Punch

- ½ cup Unsweetened coconut water
- ¼ cup Watermelon purée (strained)
- Small Mint leaf (chopped)

Serve over crushed ice in a wide-bottom bowl

Tail Wag Review:
- ☐ Licked clean
- ☐ Needed coaxing
- ☐ Turned up nose

Daiquiri Dreams & Doggy Delights

Tail Wag Review:
- ☐ Licked clean
- ☐ Needed coaxing
- ☐ Turned up nose

Cold drink. Warm sunshine. Loyal company

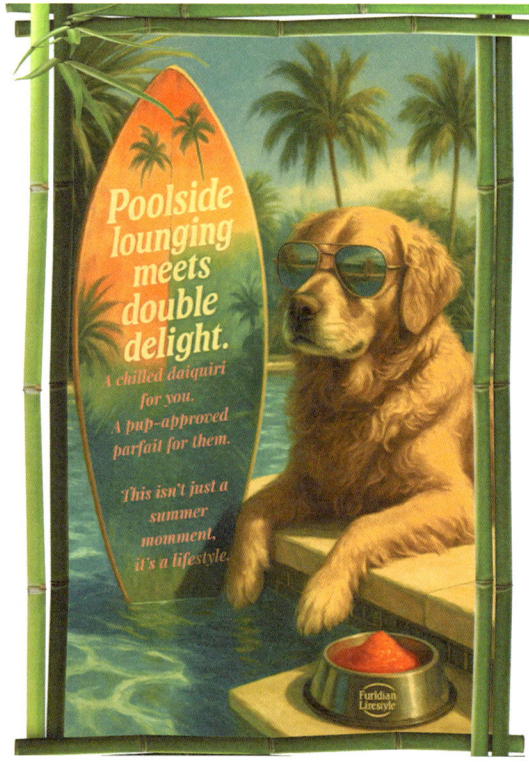

Poolside lounging meets double delight.

A chilled daiquiri for you. A pup-approved parfait for them.

This isn't just a summer momment, it's a lifestyle.

Furidian's Pool Rule #1: Stay cool. Look cooler.

Strawberry Daiquiri

Ingredients:
- 1½ oz Light Rum
- 6 oz Strawberry daiquiri Mix
- Ice

Instructions: Blend

Glassware: Chilled rocks glass

Garnish: Strawberry or Lime Wedge

🐾 Berry Good Pup

Ingredients:
- Strawberry purée
- Pup Cloud

Furidian Tip: Freeze the Berry Good Pup mix in a silicone mold for a cooling dog treat that lasts longer than your tan.

Reclaim the Quiet

> There's power in the pause. In the silence between homework, dance, and sports, find your breath, pour your peace, and sit beside the one who never rushes you.

Recess Refresher

Ingredients:
2 oz Pear juice
1 oz Chamomile tea (chilled)
½ oz Elderflower liqueur or honey syrup
1 ½ oz Vodka or Gin
Squeeze of lemon

Glassware: Coupe or stemless wine glass

Garnish: floating chamomile flower or rosemary sprig

Furidian's Pool Rule #1:
Don't let the mess steal the moment

🐾 After Bell Brew

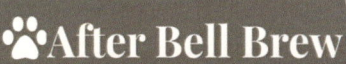

Tail Wag Review:
☐ Licked clean
☐ Needed coaxing
☐ Turned up nose

Ingredients:
1 oz Chilled chamomile tea (unsweetened)
1 oz Goat's milk
2 small frozen banana slices
Optional: sprinkle of bee pollen

Glassware: Shallow pup-safe ceramic bowl

Garnish: Dehydrated apple slice or a biscuit

Happy Hour After the Howling

Tail Wag Review:
- ☐ Licked clean
- ☐ Needed coaxing
- ☐ Turned up nose

Furidian's October Rule #1: when masks go on, your true friends stay visible

Boulevardier

Ingredients:
- 1½ oz Bourbon
- 1 oz Sweet Vermouth
- ¾ oz Blood Orange Liqueur
- 1 dash Chocolate Bitters
- Black salt or cocoa rim (optional)

Glassware: Shake all ingredients with ice, strain into a rocks glass over a single cube. Rim glass with black salt or cocoa for a moody Halloween vibe.

Garnish: burnt orange peel.

🐾 Bark & Bite Blood Bowl

Ingredients:
- ¼ cup Plain goat milk
- 1 tbsp Unsweetened beet purée or dog-safe red berry purée (for "blood" effect)
- ½ tsp Plain Greek yogurt (optional swirl on top)
- 1 tsp Coconut flakes (optional for spooky garnish)

Instructions:
Pour goat milk into a shallow bowl. Swirl in purée gently to create streaks. Top with a dollop of yogurt and sprinkle coconut flakes for a ghostly look.

Harvest Hounds & Toasted Tails

Tail Wag Review:
- ☐ Licked clean
- ☐ Needed coaxing
- ☐ Turned up nose

Like leaves in the wind, family may scatter with the season, but the roots remain deep, loyal, and unshaken."
~ *Furidian*

Furidian's Fall Rule #1: Leaves fall, standards do not

Furidian Fall Reserve

Ingredients:
- 2 oz Apple cider
- 1 oz Unsweetened pumpkin purée
- ½ oz Lemon juice
- Dash of cinnamon
- Add 1½ oz Bourbon

Glassware: Shake and pour over ice in a rocks glass.

Garnish: Cinnamon stick.

🐾 Pupkin Pumkin Spice

Ingredients:
- ½ cup Unsweetened pumpkin purée
- ¼ cup Goat's milk
- Dash of Ceylon cinnamon

Shake with ice and serve chilled in a shallow dish.

Garnish: dog treat biscuit.

The North Paw Collection

Winterberry Velvet

Ingredients:
- 2 oz Gin
- ½ oz Raspberry liquor
- ¾ oz White Vermouth
- **Splash** of peppermint Syrup

Glassware: Shake with ice and strain into Crushed peppermint rimmed martini glass

Garnish: fresh rosemary or berry skewer

Heavy pours. Heavier paws. Thick fur. Thicker coats. Welcome to winter!

Furidian's Winter Rule #1: if the fire's lit, the glass should be full

🐾 Puppermint Swirl

Tail Wag Review:
- ☐ Licked clean
- ☐ Needed coaxing
- ☐ Turned up nose

Ingredients:
- ¼ cup Plain goat milk (smooth white base)
- ½ tbsp Plain mashed strawberries or unsweetened strawberry purée (vibrant red swirl)
- ½ tsp Plain goat yogurt (adds creamy texture)
- Optional: 1 tsp coconut flakes (sprinkled on top for snow effect)
- Crushed ice or frozen into festive paw-shaped molds

Instructions:
- Pour goat milk into a clear bowl.
- Swirl in the strawberry purée gently-don't fully mix for that candy cane stripe look
- Add the goat yogurt on top like a dollop of Paw Cloud
- Sprinkle optional coconut for the snowy finish

The Spirit of the Pour:
History Meets Hospitality

LEDGER OF LIQUOR LORE

A WARNING Before We Continue

The following pages explore the history, categories, and culture of human spirits.

From here forward, this book speaks only to the human side of the bar.

These are not recipes for your dog. Alcohol is toxic to dogs and must never be served under any circumstances.

Read with curiosity.
Pour with care.

~Furidian

Furidian's Pouring Points
A Spirited History of Booze

Mead
6500-7000 BC

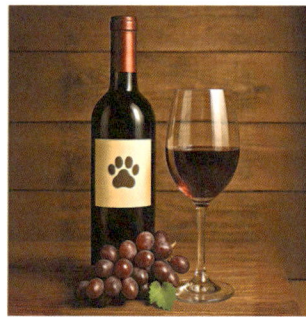

Wine
5400 BC

Beer
3400 BC

Vodka
800's AD

Brandy
1300's AD

Whiskey
1405 AD

Tequila
1600's AD

Gin
1650 AD

Rum
1700's AD

Wine
"A gentleman knows: wine isn't poured to impress, it's poured to connect."
~ Furidian

Red

Best Served In: Large-bowled red wine glass
Temperature: 60–65°F (15–18°C)
"Room temperature" for reds means slightly cooler than your living room, not the Florida sun.
Notable Varieties:
- Cabernet Sauvignon – Full-bodied, dark fruit, structured
- Merlot – Smooth, plum-forward, soft tannins
- Pinot Noir – Light, earthy, red berries
- Syrah/Shiraz – Spicy, bold, jammy
- Zinfandel – Rich, jam-like, higher alcohol

White

Best Served In: U-shaped white wine glass
Temperature: 45–55°F (7–13°C)
Chill whites and blushes in the fridge 1–2 hours before serving.
Notable Varieties:
- Chardonnay – Buttery, oaked or crisp
- Sauvignon Blanc – Zesty, grassy, citrus
- Riesling – Floral, sweet or dry
- Pinot Grigio – Light, refreshing, green apple
- Moscato – Sweet, aromatic, low alcohol

Blush

Best Served In: All-purpose or tulip glass
Temperature: 50–55°F (10–13°C)
Notable Varieties:
- White Zinfandel – Sweet, strawberry-forward
- Grenache Rosé – Crisp, red fruit
- Sangiovese Rosé – Dry, elegant, floral

Always hold wine glasses by the stem!

Sparkling Wines and Champagne

Roots and Rumors
Bubbles were once considered a flaw, wine that misbehaved in the bottle. In 17th-century France, fermentation paused in winter, then woke in spring, trapping carbon dioxide. Some bottles burst, others fizzed, and legend credits Dom Pérignon with taming the sparkle. The truth was slower, a waltz of accident and intention. In England, Christopher Merrett had already noted adding sugar to spark a second fermentation. In Champagne's chalky hills, winemakers refined the méthode champenoise, turning unruly bubbles into celebration. Soon France claimed the crown, pouring golden streams for kings, while Italy brought Prosecco's bright laughter, Spain Cava's golden warmth, and the New World bottled its own reasons to celebrate.

Map and Method
True Champagne comes only from its namesake region in northeast France, with grapes legally limited to Chardonnay (white), Pinot Noir (black), and Pinot Meunier (black). The grapes are pressed gently to keep the juice clear and avoid bitter compounds from skins, seeds, or stems. Then it is fermented into a still base wine. Sugar and yeast are added before bottling again, and a second fermentation inside the sealed glass traps carbon dioxide, creating the sparkle. The wine rests with the lees, silky spent yeast that, over months or years, adds notes of brioche, nuts, and cream while refining the bubbles. Once aging is complete, bottles are slowly rotated (riddled) so the lees settle in the neck, which is frozen, and the sediment ejected (disgorged). A final dose of wine and sugar balances the specific style before the cork and wire cage are secured. Only then is Champagne ready to meet the glass for the celebration toast.

Bottle to Bar
Serve Champagne well-chilled, around 45°F. Pour slowly down a tilted glass to preserve the mousse. Flutes showcase the bubbles; white-wine glasses unlock more aroma. Brut is the most versatile. Rosé Champagne adds red-berry charm; vintage bottles bring depth worth savoring. Prosecco offers a gentle floral sparkle, while Cava delivers crispness and value. Whether it's a prestige cuvée or a Tuesday night pour, if it's in your glass, it's the right occasion.

Furidian's Field Notes
In 2010, a bottle of Champagne salvaged from a 19th-century shipwreck in the Baltic Sea fetched over $43,000 at auction. For context, even the rarest, most coveted modern prestige cuvées rarely top $10,000. The cold, dark seabed had acted as a perfect cellar, preserving the wine for nearly two centuries. Tasters described it as surprisingly drinkable, proof that sometimes the best vintage is simply the one that survives.

Furidian's Pawtender's Pour

LAGERS
Serve cold, 38–45°F (3–7°C)

Pale Lager / Pilsner
Crisp, refreshing, golden to light amber
Example: Stella Artois, Heineken

Amber Lager
Slightly richer with toasted malt.
Example: Yuengling, Brooklyn Lager

Dark Lager / Bock
Deep color, toasty and sweet, often seasonal
Example: Shiner Bock, Dunkel

WHEAT / HEFEWEIZEN
Wheat Beer / Hefeweizen
Example: Blue Moon, Weihenstephaner

ALES
Serve warm, 45–55°F (7–13°C)

Pale Ale / IPA
Hoppy, floral, and citrus-forward.
Example: Sierra Nevada, Dogfish Head IPA

Brown Ale
Nutty, mild bitterness, malty backbone
Example: Newcastle

STOUT / PORTER
Serve 50–55°F (10–13°C)
Roasted, chocolatey, dark and smooth
Example: Guinness, Founders Porter

Pour at a 45° angle, then straighten the glass halfway to create 1–1.5 inches of foam—key for aroma and taste

Pilsner   Pint   Mug   Port   Stella

Vodka

Roots and Rumors

In the frozen borderlands where empires clashed, two nations waged a quiet war, not with swords, but with stills. Poland had gorzałka "burning water," first poured by monks in stone cellars. Russia answered with wódka, "little water," distilled from potatoes, rye, or whatever the land could spare. The names blurred in the 15th century, but the intent held steady: turn grain's last gasp into liquid survival. Gorzałka burned rough and raw. Vodka learned refinement. What started as crude medicine became a national ritual, poured in silence, carried through winters, and held in high regard. By the 1700s, vodka wasn't just a drink. It was taxed, traded, and used as currency. Soldiers carried it. States controlled it. It became a symbol of endurance: unflavored, unyielding, and unmistakably Eastern.

Map and Method

The Vodka Belt stretches cold and proud from Poland and Russia to the Baltics and Scandinavia, where harsh soil breeds hardy grains. Rye thrives in rocky ground, wheat in fertile fields, potatoes wherever they're planted. Vodka can be made from anything that ferments, but the masters don't chase shortcuts—they chase clarity. Distill to 95% ABV, cut with pure water, filter through charcoal, quartz, or silver—not to add flavor, but to remove doubt. Masters don't count distillations. They trust heat, copper, and time. The best vodkas don't erase character; they distill it down to its essence.

Bottle to Bar

Vodka enters the glass with quiet authority; clear, cold, utterly composed. In a Moscow Mule, it lays the foundation so ginger beer's fire can breathe. In a Martini, it offers pure, icy resolve. No interference. No compromise. The grain speaks in whispers: potato vodkas roll creamy and full, rye cuts sharp and bright, corn glides smooth and soft.

Vodka doesn't compete. It builds structure, then vanishes—anchoring citrus, herbs, and bitters while refusing the spotlight. In the U.S., unflavored vodka must bottle at 40% ABV minimum. Flavored vodka drops to a separate class—as low as 30% ABV. That neutrality isn't weakness. It's discipline. The invisible backbone holding every other ingredient in place, steady and unapologetic.

Furidian's Field Notes

Vodka once cleaned wounds, paid taxes, and crowned kings. In Russia, it was survival distilled from frozen earth and endless winters. Today's "Russian" vodka is mostly marketing—Smirnoff bottles in Illinois, Stoli fled Moscow years ago. For authentic taste, reach for Beluga's creamy weight, Zyr's clean bite, or Russian Standard's honest heat. Real vodka doesn't need a passport, but it should taste like it earned one. Serve it neat, cold, and with respect.

Vodka

Vodka

Name	Origin	GF	Base	Distillation	Tasting Notes
Crystal Head	Canada	🦴	Corn	4x distilled + diamond filter	Crisp, clean, no additives
Beluga	Russia	-	Malted Barley	Multi / slow-filtered	Ultra-smooth, creamy, slightly sweet
Hammer & Sickle	Russia	-	Winter Wheat	Premium Methods	clean, dry, luxurious image
Belvedere	Poland	-	Rye	4x distilled	Spicy, dry, elegant finish
Cîroc	France	🦴	Grapes	5x distilled	Silky, aromatic, subtle fruit
Grey Goose	France	-	Winter Wheat	5x distilled	Silky, soft, lightly sweet
Chopin	Poland	🦴	Potato	4x distilled	Full-bodied, creamy, clean finish
Zyr	Russia	-	Wheat & Rye	5x distilled	Velvety, bold, clean spice

Name	Origin	GF	Base	Distillation	Tasting Notes
Hangar One	USA	-	Wheat & Grape	Hybrid	Floral, balanced, light fruit
Ocean	USA	🦴	Organic Sugarcane	Multiple	Smooth, clean, subtle tropical note
Reyka	Iceland	-	Wheat & Barley	Lava rock filtered	Glacial-pure, minerally smooth
Ketel One	Netherlands	-	Wheat	Column + pot still blend	Crisp, citrusy, balanced
Effen	Netherlands	-	Wheat	Continuous	Clean, crisp, hint of vanilla
Tito's	USA	🦴	Corn	6x distilled	Neutral, clean, slight sweetness
Russian Standard	Russia	-	Wheat	Multi / charcoal filtered	Classic, clean, smooth spice
Absolut	Sweden	-	Winter Wheat	Continuous distillation	Clean, subtle spice, smooth mixer
Deep Eddy	USA	🦴	Corn	Column still	Crisp, sweet, smooth

Name	Origin	GF	Base	Distillation	Tasting Notes
Luksusowa	Poland	🦴	Potato	Triple distilled	Creamy, rich, best-value potato vodka
Stolichnaya	Latvia (originally Russia)	-	Wheat & Rye	Triple distilled	Peppery, dry, clean
Sobieski	Poland	-	Rye	Continuous	Bold, spicy, dry
Skyy	USA	🦴	Wheat	Quadruple distilled, triple filtered	Dry, peppery, mineral finish
New Amsterdam	USA	-	Grain	Column distilled	Smooth, slightly citrusy
Pinnacle	France	-	Wheat	Triple distilled	Light, mixable, soft
Svedka	Sweden	-	Wheat	Continuous distillation	Clean, smooth, lightly fruity
Smirnoff	USA/UK	🦴	Corn	3x distilled, 10x filtered	Light, mixable, budget workhorse

Whiskey

What Is Whiskey?
Whiskey is where grain meets fire and time does the rest. Born in the stone-walled monasteries of Ireland and Scotland, it traveled the world in oak and iron, adapting to the land but never losing its soul. Barley ruled the old world. Corn and rye claimed the new. The grain may change, barley, corn, rye, or wheat, but whiskey's ritual remains sacred: mash the grain, let it ferment, run it through fire, then give it a long, quiet rest in oak. Ireland's monks first wrote it down in 1405, but the craft had been burning in secret long before. As whiskey ages, barrels breathe, losing 2–5% each year to the heavens. That missing portion? Distillers call it the "angel's share." The spelling shifts with geography: "whiskey," with an "e," became standard in 19th-century Ireland to set it apart from Scotch. That tradition carried into the U.S. In Scotland, Canada, and Japan, it remains "whisky." Same craft. Same soul. Different signature.

The Process
Every whiskey follows the same ancient ritual, no matter where it's born. First comes the mashing: crushed grain meets warm water, sometimes joined by "sour mash" from yesterday's batch to keep the family line strong. Fermentation follows, as yeast transforms the mash into "wash"—a low-proof beer-like liquid that carries the spirit's raw soul. Then fire. The wash is heated until alcohol rises, condenses, and runs clear. Most whiskeys are double-distilled. Pot stills add weight and character. Column stills keep it lean and clean. Finally, oak. New spirit enters the barrel clear and comes out golden, breathing with the seasons. Two years earns the word "straight." But every whiskey needs time to find its voice.

Whiskey by World
The laws shift with borders. The soil speaks in different tongues. But whiskey's bones stay the same: grain, fire, oak, and time.

Bourbon: America's charred oak anthem—sweet corn, vanilla fire, and new barrel pride.
American Rye: Bold and spice-driven, where pepper meets grain and neither backs down.
Scotch: Born in Highland mist. Smoky, complex, aged in borrowed barrels, built to haunt your memory.
Irish: Triple-distilled smoothness with honeyed grain and gentle spice, rebellion refined.
Canadian: The diplomat's whisky, blended for balance, aged in cold patience.
Japanese: Precision distilled into poetry. Delicate smoke, mountain water, silk over steel.

Bourbon

Roots and Rumors
Bourbon wasn't born in a palace. It was raised in rebellion, sweat, and Appalachian smoke. In the late 1700s, Scotch-Irish settlers brought their stills to the American frontier. Faced with excess corn and government taxes, they adapted, distilling corn mash and aging it in charred oak barrels. Whether by accident or instinct, the result was something new: a spirit mellowed by wood, layered with vanilla, spice, and fire. It took its name from Bourbon County, stamped on barrels shipped downriver to New Orleans. By the time they reached the docks, the whiskey had picked up a color, a voice, and a reputation. It wasn't just whiskey anymore. It was Bourbon. Bold, native, and unmistakably American.

Map and method
To wear the name bourbon, whiskey must follow America's strictest rules. Made in the U.S. with at least 51% corn. Distilled to no more than 160 proof. Aged in new, charred American oak at 125 proof or less. Bottled at a minimum of 80 proof. No additives. No shortcuts. Just grain, fire, and time. Bourbon must age, but not forever. A two-year minimum earns it the word "straight." Four years under one distiller, one season, and bottled at 100 proof? That's bottled-in-bond, and it means someone's watching. Kentucky became bourbon's spiritual home through geology, not just tradition. Its limestone-rich water filters out iron and adds a soft, clean finish. That pure water, fresh oak, and Southern climate with hot summers pushing whiskey deep into wood, cool winters pulling it back. A process that transforms what goes in clear, comes out rich, structured, and unmistakably amber colored bourbon.

Bottle to Bar
Bourbon shows up strong, no matter the glass. In cocktails like the Old Fashioned, it brings structure and warmth. Sipped neat, it opens slowly, first caramel, then toasted oak, and a finish that lingers like a well-told story. The mash bill plays its part: higher rye brings spice and snap, while wheated bourbons mellow into round, sweet finishes. Age deepens the profile. A four-year bourbon is bold and assertive. A twelve-year brings polish, restraint, and layered complexity. High-proof bottles carry weight and demand attention. But whether it's mixed, sipped, or studied, every pour is a conversation between corn, char, and time, and bourbon always speaks clearly.

Furidian's Field Notes
Bourbon doesn't borrow barrels, it breaks them in. By law, it gets first crack at brand-new charred oak, and you can taste the difference. That signature sweetness? That's fresh fire meeting raw wood. Once bourbon's done, the barrel moves on to age tequila, Scotch, or even Tabasco. But bourbon always leaves its mark. It doesn't follow. It leads.

American Whiskey

Roots and Rumors
American whiskey took shape on the frontier after Irish, Scottish, and German distillers met New World grain. Corn thrived in the South, rye in the Mid-Atlantic and Northeast. The 1791 Whiskey Tax pushed production west into Kentucky and Tennessee, where sour-mash methods and new, charred oak made the style its own. From farm stills to commercial distilleries, the hallmark became bold grain character shaped by fresh oak and time.

Map and Method
American whiskey isn't a style; it's a family reunion where everyone argues but still drinks together. Rye demands a 51% minimum grain bill and brings the spice. Corn whiskey stays sweet, often unaged, skipping new oak entirely. Tennessee whiskey runs through sugar maple charcoal with the Lincoln County Process, smoothing rough edges before barrel aging. American single malts borrow Scotland's 100% malted barley but speak pure American: some age in new oak, others in wine or bourbon barrels. Laws shift from Indiana's industrial blends to Texas heat-aged rebels, but the foundation holds: grain, fire, fermentation, oak.

Bottle to Bar
American whiskey speaks in many accents. Rye hits sharp and spicy, perfect in a Manhattan or Sazerac. Rittenhouse and High West lead the charge. Corn whiskey stays raw, clear, and criminally underrated. Tennessee whiskey drinks smooth, charcoal-filtered clean. American single malts are new but bold, Scotch-inspired, off-script, and unapologetically American. Some bottles are young and loud, others, aged deep. No matter the pour, there's something honest in the glass.

Furidian's Field Notes
American whiskey doesn't follow tradition. It builds its own and burns the rest. One barrel might taste like maple smoke and river stone; the next, like pepper and peach cobbler. It's a category built by bootstraps, shaped by soil, and bold enough to contradict itself. Whether bottled in bond or blended in a barn, it still howls the same truth: flavor follows freedom. The spelling may match Ireland's, but the spirit is pure frontier.

 *Irish Whiskey*

Roots and Rumors

Irish whiskey begins where myth meets flame. Monks returning from southern Europe brought alchemical secrets and turned them toward grain. They called it *uisce beatha*, "water of life," and by the 12th century, Irish hands had mastered the art. By the 1800s, Ireland ruled the whiskey world, Dublin and Cork distilleries supplied two-thirds of the global market. Then the empire struck back. War, tariffs, and Prohibition crushed hundreds of distilleries into a handful of survivors. The Irish spirit never died, however. It waited in cellars and memory, patient as stone. Today it rises again, carrying not just history in the glass, but the taste of a land that refuses to surrender.

Map and Method

To be called Irish whiskey, it must be mashed, distilled, and aged in Ireland for at least three years and a day in wooden casks, often ex-bourbon, sherry, or wine barrels. Most expressions are triple distilled in copper pot stills or column stills, giving Irish whiskey its signature smoothness. There are four main styles: **Single Malt** (made from 100% malted barley, produced by a single distillery), **Single Pot Still** (a uniquely Irish blend of malted and unmalted barley), **Grain Whiskey** (typically corn-based, produced in continuous stills), and **Blended Whiskey**, the most common style. Unlike Scotch, peat is rare, which results in a cleaner profile. Whether bold or subtle, Irish whiskey is shaped by restraint. The method favors grace over fire.

Bottle to Bar

Irish whiskey is a study in balance. Light-bodied and smooth, it offers notes of honey, toasted grain, baked fruit, and soft spice. Triple distillation rounds the edges, making it easy in cocktails and steady when served neat. Blends like Jameson bring versatility. Redbreast adds depth. Red Spot delivers wine-cask complexity. Bushmills, Green Spot, Teeling, Knappogue, each one speaks in its own accent, tied to place and method. Whether beside a pint or by a fire, Irish whiskey doesn't shout. It speaks gently, but with conviction.

Furidian's Field Notes

Bushmills holds the title of the world's oldest licensed distillery, its charter granted in 1608. By the 19th century, Irish whiskey was the world's drink of choice, until war, tariffs, and Prohibition brought it to its knees. Unlike Scotch producers, Irish distillers refused to deal with American bootleggers, and others filled the gap. Smooth, peat-free whiskey became Ireland's signature, but today, a new generation is bringing the smoke back, quietly, patiently. A well-made pot still whiskey doesn't shout. It lingers. One sip, and the story stays with you.

Bourbon

Name	Region	Grain Profile	ABV	Tasting Notes	Age
Pappy Van Winkle	Wheated Bourbon	Corn, wheat, barley	~45%	Caramel, oak, dried fruit, spice	15 Years
Stagg Jr.	Barrel Proof Bourbon	Corn, rye, barley	~63%	Rich spice, dark fruit, cinnamon	NAS
Blanton's	Single Barrel Bourbon	Corn, rye, barley	~46%	Vanilla, nutmeg, caramel, orange zest	NAS
Angel's Envy	Port Cask Finished Bourbon	Corn, rye, barley	43%	Dark fruit, maple, spice, port wine finish	NAS
Woodford Reserve	Kentucky Straight Bourbon	Corn, rye, barley	45%	Citrus, cinnamon, cocoa, toffee	NAS
Knob Creek	Small Batch Bourbon	Corn, rye, barley	50%	Vanilla, toasted oak, nutmeg	9 Years
Maker's Mark	Wheated Bourbon	Corn, wheat, barley	45%	Sweet vanilla, caramel, soft spice	NAS
Jim Beam	Kentucky	Corn, rye, barley	40%	Oak, vanilla, nutty, mild sweetness	NAS

American Whiskey

Name	Region	Type	Grain Profile	ABV	Tasting Notes	Age
WhistlePig PiggyBack 6 Year	Vermont	Rye	100% Straight Rye	48%	Spice, citrus, black pepper, leather	6 Years
Jack Daniel's Single Barrel Select	Tennessee	Tennessee	Corn, Rye, Malted Barley-Charcoal Mellowed	47%	Caramel, spice, toasted oak, vanilla	No Age Statement
High West Campfire	Utah	Blended	Unique blend: Bourbon, Rye, Peated Scotch	46%	Honey, smoke, spice, dried fruit	Blend of Ages
George Dickel 12 Year	Tennessee	Tennessee	Corn, Rye, Malted Barley-Charcoal Mellowed	45%	Vanilla, maple, nuts, oak	12 Years
Stranahan's Single Barrel	Colorado	Single Malt	100% malted barley-Craft Single Malt	~47%	Toasted oak, caramel, dark chocolate, dried fruit, leather, spice	4-7 years (varies)
Jack Daniel's Old No. 7	Tennessee	Tennessee	Corn, Rye, Malted Barley-Charcoal Mellowed	40%	Vanilla, caramel, banana, charred oak	No Age Statement
Seagram's 7 Crown	USA	Blended	Neutral Grain Spirits + Whiskey Blen	40%	Light vanilla, honey, grain, mellow	No Age Statement

Irish Whiskey

Name	Region	Type	Grain Profile	Tasting Notes	Aging
Redbreast 12 Year	Midleton, Cork	Single Pot Still	Malted + Unmalted Barley	Rich sherry, nuts, spice	12 Years
Teeling Small Batch	Dublin	Blended	Corn, Malted Barley	Vanilla, rum sweetness, spice	No Age Statement
Green Spot	Midleton, Cork	Single Pot Still	Malted + Unmalted Barley	Green apple, clove, honey	7-10 Years (approx.)
Writers' Tears	Carlow	Blended	Malted Barley + Grain	Floral, sweet grain, soft spice	No Age Statement
Jameson Black Barrel	Midleton, Cork	Blended	Pot Still + Grain	Butterscotch, nutmeg, vanilla	NAS (approx. 8-12 Years)
Powers Gold Label	Midleton, Cork	Single Pot Still	Malted + Unmalted Barley	Spicy, robust, cereal grain	NAS (approx. 6-7 Years)
Bushmills 10 Year	Bushmills, Antrim	Single Malt	100% Malted Barley	Honey, fruit, oak	10 Years
Tullamore D.E.W.	Tullamore	Blended	Malt, Grain, Pot Still	Malty, citrus, toffee	No Age Statement
Jameson Original	Midleton, Cork	Blended	Malt, Grain, Pot Still	Light floral, toasted wood, vanilla	No Age Statement

 # Scotch

Roots and Rumors
In 1494, Friar John Cor was caught red-handed distilling "aqua vitae" for King James IV, the first whisky bootlegger in recorded history. For centuries, monks had been turning grain into medicine, ritual, and quiet rebellion. The 1707 Union with England brought crushing taxes, driving distillers into Highland caves and clan-run smuggling routes. Scotch survived underground until the 1823 Excise Act dragged it into daylight. By century's end, Johnnie Walker, Chivas, and Dewar's had conquered the world, turning Highland moonshine into global liquid gold. From monks to outlaws to royal warrants, Scotch carries five centuries of rebellion in every bottle.

Map and Method
Scotch lives by Scotland's rules: mashed, distilled, and aged entirely on Scottish soil for a minimum of three years in oak casks—usually ex-bourbon, sherry, or wine barrels. Malted barley or mixed grains, fermented with yeast, distilled below 94.8% ABV. No additives except caramel coloring. Bottled at a minimum of 40% ABV. Five official categories define the family: **Single Malt** (100% malted barley, one distillery, pot stills). **Single Grain** (other grains, one distillery, continuous stills). **Blended Malt** (single malts from multiple distilleries). **Blended Grain** (single-grain whiskies blended). **Blended Scotch** (the most common, balancing malt and grain). The categories may shift, but the ritual doesn't. Scotch demands patience, precision, and Scottish soil.

Bottle to Bar
Scotch isn't built for speed. Whether sipped neat or opened with water to unlock hidden oils, a good Scotch unfolds slowly. The barrel always leaves its mark. Ex-bourbon, sherry, or wine casks lend vanilla, dried fruit, and spice. Islay brings peat and brine: Laphroaig, Ardbeg. Speyside offers orchard fruit and honey: Glenfiddich, Balvenie. Highlands stretch from floral to smoky. Each region speaks its own dialect. Scotch isn't a shot. It's a slow conversation. Every pour carries centuries of weather, wood, and care.

Furidian's Field Notes
They say the first still in Scotland wasn't built; it was found, steaming in a cave beneath Ben Lomond, left behind by the fae. Highlanders believe distillers aren't taught but chosen, marked at birth by the scent of peat smoke on their skin. At Glenfiddich, pipers still play to the barrels: a 300-year tradition meant to bless the whisky and calm its spirit. On Islay, some swear selkies sing to the seaside casks, giving them their briny soul. Elsewhere, peat is still harvested by hand, block by block, cut from the land like stone. In Scotland, whisky isn't manufactured. It's coaxed from fire, fog, water, and whispered legend.

Canadian Whisky

Roots and Rumors

Canadian whisky was born from winter and necessity. After the American Revolution, loyalists carried rye seed and copper stills north, distilling rough spirits to survive the cold. Malcolm MacLeod, a Scottish settler, is said to have discovered whisky's mellowing magic during the freeze-thaw cycles of 1783. By the 1800s, Hiram Walker refined the process: aging longer, blending cleaner, and shipping smoother whisky far beyond the border. When Queen Victoria declared Walker's whisky "exceptionally fine" in 1858, Canada found not just its crown, but its character. Not bold like bourbon. Not peated like Scotch. Canadian whisky offers something quieter: patient, blended, and frost-tempered with grace.

Map and Method

Canadian whisky plays by looser rules than its neighbors. Mashed, distilled, and aged in Canada for a minimum of three years in small wooden barrels; new or used, charred or not. Bottled at 40% ABV minimum. Most producers distill each grain separately: corn for sweetness, rye for spice, wheat or barley for texture. Then they blend like painters mixing colors. Up to 9.09% can legally include other aged spirits, wine, or flavoring agents for consistency. And while "rye whisky" appears on the label, there's no legal minimum for rye content. It's tradition over chemistry, craft over rules.

Bottle to Bar

Canadian whisky is light, smooth, and versatile. Expect soft oak, vanilla, dried fruit, and gentle rye spice: ideal for highballs, clean cocktails, or a quiet sip neat. But smooth doesn't mean simple. High-rye expressions like Lot No. 40 and Alberta Premium Cask Strength bring bold pepper, dry oak, and real grip. Even WhistlePig's acclaimed rye began with Canadian distillate. During Prohibition, brands like Canadian Club and Crown Royal became bootleg staples, building a quiet legacy across the border. Today, Canada continues to produce world-class whisky, shaped by cold air, slow aging, and a steady hand.

Furidian's Field Notes

They say Canada's winters age whisky in dog years, each freeze-thaw cycle pulling flavor deeper into the wood. During Prohibition, whisky crossed frozen lakes on sleds and decoy boats, slipping past U.S. agents under the cover of snow. Crown Royal was first bottled in 1939 to honor a royal visit, and it never left the throne. Canadian Club earned its street cred running underground from Windsor to Detroit, fueling Capone's empire. Most Canadian whiskies aim for balance, but don't be fooled: a good cask-strength pour still hits hard enough to melt a snowbank.

Japanese Whisky

Roots and Rumors
Smoke whispers drifted from Scotland to Japan in the early 1900s, but what began as an apprenticeship became mastery. Masataka Taketsuru, a young chemist, studied distillation in Scotland's Highlands and carried its secrets across the world. In 1923, Yamazaki distillery opened its doors, and Japan began writing its own whisky language: disciplined, delicate, reverent. Inspired by Scottish tradition but shaped by mountain mist, native oak, and obsessive precision, Japanese whisky became something entirely new: liquid meditation distilled into bottles.

Map and Method
Japan drew its lines in 2021, demanding every drop calling itself Japanese whisky earn its name on home soil. Mashed, fermented, distilled, aged (minimum three years), and bottled entirely in Japan using domestic water and at least some malted grain. Aging happens in wooden casks no larger than 700 liters. No additives except caramel coloring. Production mirrors Scotch: barley dominates, corn and rye support grain whisky. Double distillation in pot stills is common; column stills handle grain spirits. But unlike Scotland's trading culture, Japanese distilleries blend only their own stock, building identity from within. Japan's extreme seasons accelerate the process. Blazing summers push whisky deep into casks, bitter winters pull it back. The result? Complexity earned quickly but never rushed.

Bottle to Bar
Japanese whisky doesn't shout; it whispers with purpose. Expect balance over bite: soft orchard fruit, floral lift, honeyed grain, and precise spice. Peat, when used, stays subtle: measured, never dominant. Hibiki blends like a half-remembered dream: layered, graceful, restrained. Yamazaki 12 brings orchard warmth and cedar with a breath of smoke. Hakushu stays crisp, herbal, mountain bright. Nikka From the Barrel packs bold spice into compact quiet strength. These aren't spirits for speed or shortcuts. Good Japanese whisky demands patience and budget. Real bottles have become liquid gold, but the experience justifies the cost. Serve neat or over a single cube and let the silence carry the rest.

Furidian's Field Notes
Mizunara oak is Japan's most stubborn gift to whisky. It warps. It leaks. It takes decades to mature. But inside its grain lives something rare. Those who dare to age their spirit in it are rewarded with notes of sandalwood, incense, coconut, and quiet spice. It doesn't just make whisky better. It makes it unforgettable.

SCOTCH

CANADIAN

JAPANESE

Scotch

Name	Region	Category	Grain Profile	Peat Level	Tasting Notes	Aging
Macallan 25	Speyside	Single Malt	100% Malted Barley	None	Rich & sherried dried fruit, spice, oak	25 Years
Johnnie Walker Blue	Blended (Various)	Blended	Malted Barley + Grain	Low	Smooth & balanced vanilla, honey, dried fruit	No Age Statement
Lagavulin 16	Islay	Single Malt	100% Malted Barley	High	Smoke, seaweed, iodine	16 Years
Oban 14	Highlands	Single Malt	100% Malted Barley	Light	Coastal & lightly peated brine, citrus, smoke	14 Years
Glenlivet 12	Speyside	Single Malt	100% Malted Barley	None	Fruity & floral apple, honey, floral	12 Years
Glenfiddich 12	Speyside	Single Malt	100% Malted Barley	None	Fruity & fresh pear, malt, oak	12 Years
Chivas Regal 12	Blended (Various)	Blended	Malted Barley + Grain	Low	Balanced & mellow toffee, vanilla, spice	12 Years
Monkey Shoulder	Speyside	Blended Malt	100% Malted Barley	None	Smooth & mellow creamy malt, vanilla, fruit	No Age Statement
Dewar's 12	Blended (Various)	Blended	Malted Barley + Grain	Light	Lightly smoky & sweet honey, smoke, vanilla	12 Years

Canadian Whisky

Name	Type	ABV	Tasting Notes	Distillery	Aging	Grain Profile
Wiser's 18 Year	Blended	40%	Caramel, vanilla, oak, spice, smooth finish	Hiram Walker	18 Years	Malted Barley + Corn + Rye
Lot No. 40	Rye	43%	Bold rye spice, toffee, dried fruit, oak	Hiram Walker	-	100% Rye
Pike Creek	Blended (Port Barrel Finish)	42%	Dried fruit, spice, sweetness from port finish	Hiram Walker	10 Years	Corn + Rye + Malted Barley
Collingwood	Blended (Maplewood Stave Finish)	40%	Smooth, sweet, toasted maple, light oak	Canadian Mist	-	Corn + Rye + Malted Barley
Crown Royal	Blended	40%	Vanilla, fruit, light spice, creamy finish	Crown Royal (Diageo)	-	Corn + Rye + Malted Barley
Canadian Club 100% Rye	Rye	40%	Spicy rye, green apple, butterscotch, oak	Canadian Club	-	100% Rye
Seagram's VO	Blended	40%	Light oak, vanilla, soft grain sweetness	Seagram (Pernod Ricard)	~6 Years	Corn + Rye + Barley

Japanes Whisky

Name	Distillery		Type	ABV	Tasting Notes	Aging
Yamazaki 18 Year	Yamazaki Distillery (Suntory), Shimamoto, Japan	Japan's oldest whisky distillery, founded by Suntory in 1923.	Single Malt	43%	Rich dried fruits, dark chocolate, espresso, aged sherry wood, and elegant smoke.	18 Years
Hibiki 21 Year	Yamazaki Distillery (Suntory), Shimamoto, Japan	Produced with pure mountain water in Kyoto Prefecture.	Blended	43%	Plum compote, sandalwood, spiced oak, black tea, and long, silky sweetness.	21 Years
Yamazaki 12 Year	Blend of Yamazaki, Hakushu, and Chita Distilleries	Blended at Suntory, using malt from Yamazaki & Hakushu, grain from Chita.	Single Malt	43%	Ripe peach, pineapple, warm cedar, gentle smoke, and vanilla bean.	12 Years
Hibiki Japanese Harmony	Blend of Yamazaki, Hakushu, and Chita Distilleries	Famous Suntory blend, malt from Yamazaki & Hakushu, grain from Chita.	Blended	43%	Orange peel, white chocolate, rosewater, mizunara spice, and a clean floral lift.	3+
Nikka From the Barrel	Yoichi & Miyagikyo Distilleries, Japan	Blend of malt from Yoichi & Miyagikyo, grain from Miyagikyo.	Blended	51%	Bold spice, dried apricot, toffee, charred oak, and a warm peppery finish.	3+
Toki (Suntory)	Blend of Yamazaki, Hakushu, and Chita Distilleries	Created from all three Suntory distilleries.	Blended	43%	Crisp green apple, fresh basil, white grape, honey, and a hint of vanilla oak.	3+

Tequila

Roots and Rumors
Tequila begins in volcanic soil and myth. Long before copper stills arrived, Indigenous peoples of central Mexico fermented agave into pulque: milky, sacred, and slow. Then came 1521, and with the Spanish came distillation. Don Pedro Sánchez de Tagle, often called the "Father of Tequila," merged Old World technique with native wisdom. In the shadow of the Tequila volcano, roasted agave hearts met fire, and a clear spirit ran into clay cups. But tequila wasn't invented; it was revealed, over centuries of labor, ritual, and volcanic patience.

Map and Method
True tequila belongs to five designated regions of Mexico, with Jalisco as its volcanic heart. By law, premium tequila must be 100% Blue Weber agave: no shortcuts, no substitutes. The ritual begins with jimadores harvesting piñas by hand, each one weighing 80 to 200 pounds of concentrated agave sugar. Slow roasted in brick ovens or modern autoclaves, the hearts release their earthy sweetness. Crush, ferment, distill twice, usually in copper stills that preserve character. Blanco bottles young and fierce. Reposado rests in oak for two to twelve months, gaining mellow depth. Añejo ages one to three years, drawing vanilla and spice from wood. Extra Añejo pushes beyond three years into liquid luxury. Highland tequilas lean floral and fruit-forward. Lowland expressions stay earthy, mineral driven. The soil writes the story; time reveals it.

Bottle to Bar
Tequila deserves better than shots and salt; it's a precision spirit. A good Blanco can rival vodka for clarity, but leaves behind the warmth of roasted agave. Reposado belongs in an Old Fashioned. Añejo is built for the fireside. Bring in mezcal, tequila's smoky, wild cousin, and suddenly the bar becomes a journey through Mexico's soul. Whether shaken into a Margarita or sipped neat from a clay copita, tequila demands attention. It speaks of land, labor, and a little rebellion. And the best ones? They don't burn. They bloom.

Furidian's Field Notes
Real tequila jimadores can tell an agave's sugar content just by thumping the piña with a wooden bat; it rings differently when it's ready. The best distilleries still use volcanic stone tahonas: massive wheels that crush agave more slowly than modern machines, releasing oils that steel blades miss. That "worm" in cheap mezcal bottles? It's actually a moth larva, and it was never traditional, just a 1940s marketing gimmick that worked too well. True tequila never needs a worm. It's got enough character on its own.

Tequila

If it says "Gold" but doesn't say "100% Agave," it's just a dressed-up mixto trying to skip the work. A real tequila earns its color in oak — not in a lab.

Tequila

Brand	Region	Blanco	Reposado	Añejo
Tears of Llorona	Jalisco	N/A	N/A	Chocolate, toffee, dried fruit, oak
Clase Azul	Jalisco (Los Altos)	Vanilla, hazelnut, cinnamon, and cream	Caramel, hazelnut, toasted oak	Toffee, fig, spice
Avión Reserva 44	Jesus Maria, Jalisco	N/A	Espresso, vanilla, warm spice	Maple, dried fruit, warm spice
Código 1530	Amatitán, Jalisco	Agave, vanilla, cocoa, oak	Vanilla, spice, mild oak	Cocoa, nutmeg, dried fruit
Cincoro	Jalisco (Multiple Regions)	Smooth, vanilla, toasted oak	Toasted oak, dried fruit, cinnamon	Cinnamon, dried fruit, vanilla

Brand	Region	Blanco	Reposado	Añejo
Casa Dragones	Tequila, Jalisco	Fresh herb, green apple, pepper	N/A	N/A
Don Julio	Atotonilco El Alto, Jalisco	Crisp agave, citrus, hints of spice	Vanilla, citrus, nutmeg	Toffee, almond, dry spice
Volcán De Mi Tierra	Lowlands and Highlands Blend	Fresh agave, citrus, light spice	Cooked agave, light pepper	Toasted oak, vanilla, pepper
Fortaleza	Tequila Valley	Olive, black pepper, citrus	Brine, citrus, butter	Citrus, cream, butter
Casamigos	Jalisco (Highlands)	Vanilla, caramel, spice	Caramel, fruit, sweet spice	Toasted vanilla, roasted agave
Patrón	Atotonilco El Alto	Citrus, white pepper, light oak	Vanilla, herbal, citrus	Oak, citrus, sweet pepper

Brand	Region	Blanco	Reposado	Añejo
El Tequileño	Tequila	Agave, citrus, light pepper	Oak, citrus, mild spice	Mature agave, light vanilla
Jose Cuervo	Tequila, Jalisco	Earthy agave, oak, pepper	Toasted agave, baking spice	Oak, vanilla, black pepper
Espolòn	Los Altos	Tropical fruit, pepper, roasted agave	Roasted pineapple, pepper	Rich spice, tropical fruit
Olmeca Altos Plata	Los Altos, Jalisco	Herbal, citrus, smooth agave	Oak, citrus, mellow spice	Spiced oak, mild citrus

| Unaged (<2 mo) | 2-12 mo | 1-3 yrt | 3+ yr | Not aged / Caramel coloring |

 Gin

Roots and Rumors
Gin began as medicine in 17th-century Holland, where Dutch physician Franciscus Sylvius infused spirits with juniper to cure internal ailments. Soldiers returning from battle called it "Dutch Courage" and brought it home to England, where it spiraled. By the 1700s, gin flooded London. It was cheap, strong, and everywhere. Addiction soared. The government blamed it for poverty, crime, and broken homes, especially among working-class mothers, earning it the name "Mother's Ruin." Laws and licensing eventually tamed the chaos. Over time, craft caught up to the madness.

Map and Method
Gin starts with neutral spirit: wheat, barley, or corn, then gets reborn through botanical redistillation. Juniper must lead. No exceptions. Distillation happens through maceration, vapor infusion, or both. The goal isn't neutrality like vodka; it's botanical clarity where each note earns its place. Styles define the family: London Dry stays crisp and bone-dry with no additives. New Western honors juniper but lets cucumber, rose, or cardamom steal scenes. Plymouth remains softer, earthier, legally tied to its English hometown. Old Tom brings Victorian sweetness back from the dead.

Bottle to Bar
Gin is the bartender's tool of choice when clarity matters. It holds shape in a Martini; grips bitter in a Negroni and turns tonic into ritual. Most gins are bottled between 40 to 47% ABV. Some legacy brands maintain higher proof through regulatory exemptions, and it shows. Dry gins snap clean and sharp. Contemporary styles flirt with florals, herbs, and citrus without losing their juniper backbone. Proof matters, but precision matters more. No spirit rewards perfect proportions, or punishes sloppy ones, quite like gin.

Furidian's Field Notes
The British Navy mixed gin with lime to fight scurvy: half tonic, half survival, and called it medicine. The result? The Gimlet. It is said that Churchill liked his Martinis so dry, he just looked at the bottle of vermouth. During Prohibition, Americans made so much bootleg gin in actual bathtubs that "bathtub gin" became synonymous with homemade liquor. The real imported gin was smuggled in coffins, hidden in hollowed-out books, and served in teacups at speakeasies. Flappers, jazz, and backroom deals: gin fueled an entire underground culture. It survived government bans, moral crusades, and shifting cocktail trends. Gin doesn't follow fashion. It sets it. The best bottles still taste like well-dressed rebellion.

 # Gin

Gin

Name	Region	Style	ABV	Tasting Notes
Monkey 47	Germany	Dry Gin	47%	Complex, herbal, citrus-forward
Ki No Bi	Japan	Japanese Dry	45.70%	Yuzu, green tea, sansho pepper
Generous Gin	France	Floral Gin	44%	Floral, citrus, smooth
Aviation	USA	American Dry	42%	Lavender, cardamom, anise
The Botanist	Scotland	Islay Dry Gin	46%	Herbal, floral, earthy
Empress 1908	Canada	Contemporary	42.50%	Butterfly pea flower, grapefruit, juniper
Hendrick's	Scotland	Cucumber Infused	41.40%	Cucumber, rose, juniper
Tanqueray No. Ten	UK	London Dry	47.30%	Citrus, juniper, smooth
Elephant Gin	Germany	London Dry	45%	Apple, pine, exotic spices

Name	Region	Style	ABV	Tasting Notes
Citadelle	France	London Dry	44%	Juniper, citrus, floral
Plymouth Gin	England	Plymouth	41.20%	Earthy, citrus, balanced
Beefeater 24	England	London Dry	45%	Tea, citrus, juniper
Sipsmith London Dry	England	London Dry	41.60%	Spicy, juniper, classic
Roku Gin	Japan	Japanese Dry	43%	Sakura, yuzu, green tea
Hayman's	England	London Dry	41.20%	Citrus, spice, traditional
Barr Hill	USA	Old Tom	45%	Honey, soft juniper, smooth

Name	Region	Style	ABV	Tasting Notes
Fords Gin	England	London Dry	45%	Citrus, coriander, soft
Bombay Sapphire	England	London Dry	47%	Coriander, lemon peel, pepper
Brokers	England	London Dry	47%	Juniper, nutmeg, spice
Beefeater	England	London Dry	44%	Juniper, citrus, bold
New Amsterdam	USA	Contemporary	40%	Citrus, sweet, smooth
Bluecoat	USA	American Dry	47%	Citrus, earthy, peppery
McCormick	USA	Value Gin	40%	Neutral, basic botanicals

Rum

Roots and Rumors

Rum began in 17th-century Barbados, not from sugar, but from its shadow. Molasses, thick and black, was considered waste. Planters fed it to livestock or let it rot. But in the tropical heat, something ancient stirred. It bubbled, fermented, and transformed. Enslaved Africans, forced to work the sugar plantations but drawing on ancestral distilling knowledge, transformed molasses into "kill-devil": fiery, crude, and powerful. Pirates drank it to steady their hands on cutlass hilts. Naval officers found that it outlasted beer in the tropics and made it official: a daily ration for every sailor. From waste to weapon to ration, rum earned its place, drop by blazing drop.

Map and Method

Rum starts with sugar: either fresh cane juice or molasses. Then it is fermented and distilled in warm coastal climates where tropical heat accelerates everything. Most rums are column-distilled for efficiency, though pot stills survive for richer, traditional styles.

The range runs wide: Light rum (also called white or silver) gets filtered, bottled young, and built for citrus cocktails. Gold rum picks up vanilla and color from brief oak aging. Dark rum ages longer, soaking up char and spice for a fuller body. Spiced and flavored rums get infused after distillation: usually sweet, often low-proof, and always obvious. The Caribbean remains rum's epicenter: Puerto Rico leads in volume, Jamaica in funk, Barbados in heritage. Tropical aging works fast; three years can accomplish what takes ten in cooler climates. In rum, time works overtime.

Bottle to Bar

Rum earns its place by doing what others won't: it adapts. Light rum cuts clean in a Daiquiri. Dark rum brings depth to a Mai Tai or Dark 'n' Stormy. Aged rum stands alone: neat, no garnish, no apology. Spiced and flavored rums sell easily but drink softly: low proof, high sugar, and more marketing than muscle. The real bottles earn their darkness from time and barrel, not caramel coloring. In rum, color lies. What matters is heat, time, and what the wood whispers back.

Furidian's Field Notes

The British Navy's daily rum ration ended on July 31, 1970—a date still mourned as "Black Tot Day." Sailors received half a pint of overproof rum daily for over 300 years until modern warfare made drunk sailors a liability. Real aged rum loses 8 to 10% to evaporation annually in tropical heat compared to just 2% for whiskey in Scotland. This evaporated loss is what distillers call the "angels' share." That's why a 12-year Caribbean rum is rarer than 18-year Scotch. The angels drink faster in paradise.

Rum

Rum

Name	Category	Region	Age	Style	Tasting Notes
Clément Canne Bleue	White	Martinique	Unaged	Rhum Agricole	Floral, grassy, clean finish
Diplomático Planas	White	Venezuela	6 Years	Charcoal-filtered Aged	Creamy, coconut, butter
Ron Zacapa XO	Dark	Guatemala	6-25 Years (Solera)	Solera-aged	Vanilla, nuts, raisin, sherry
Foursquare 2009	Dark	Barbados	10 Years	Pot & Column Still	Dry, oak, spice, leather
Chairman's Reserve Spiced	Spiced	St. Lucia	Blend	Natural Spiced	Clove, citrus peel, cinnamon
Don Q Oak Barrel Spiced	Spiced	Puerto Rico	3-6 Years	Natural Spiced	Vanilla, nutmeg, dry finish

Name	Category	Region	Age	Style	Tasting Notes
El Dorado 3 Year	White	Guyana	3 Years	Demerara	Creamy, citrus, light molasses
Probitas	White	Barbados/Jamaican	Blend	Pot & Column Blend	Banana, citrus, cane, dry finish
Appleton Estate 8 Year	Dark	Jamaica	8 Years	Pot/Column Blend	Tropical fruit, oak, spice
Mount Gay Black Barrel	Dark	Barbados	Blend	Double Char Finish	Vanilla, toasted oak, spice
Sailor Jerry	Spiced	US Virgin Islands	No Age Statement	High-proof Spiced	Vanilla, cinnamon, bold
Kraken Black Spiced	Spiced	Trinidad & Tobago	No Age Statement	Dark Spiced	Molasses, clove, rich

Name	Category	Region	Age	Style	Tasting Notes
Flor de Caña 4 ExtraSeco	White	Nicaragua	4 Years	Column Still	Dry, clean, subtle citrus
Bacardí Superior	White	Puerto Rico	1-2 Years	Charcoal Filtered	Vanilla, almond, soft citrus
Myers's Original Dark	Dark	Jamaica	Blend	Molasses-Based	Heavy molasses, caramel, smoky
Plantation Original Dark	Dark	Barbados/Jamaica	Blend	Blended Dark	Banana, spice, rich body
Captain Morgan Spiced	Spiced	Puerto Rico	No Age Statement	Mainstream Spiced	Sweet, vanilla, smooth
Blackheart Spiced Rum	Spiced	USA	No Age Statement	Budget Spiced	Vanilla, cherry, cinnamon

 *Cachaça*

Roots and Rumors

Before Brazil was Brazil, sugarcane had already taken root. Portuguese colonists brought the stalks, but it was the enslaved and the Indigenous who fermented the future. What bubbled up wasn't rum: it was something wilder, sharper, and uniquely Brazilian. Cachaça wasn't made to impress kings. It was made to survive them. Sipped by rebels, banned by royal decree, and buried in samba and street protests, cachaça carries the pulse of a nation. You don't just drink it; you taste 500 years of resistance, poured neat and proud.

Map and Method

By law, cachaça must come from Brazil and be made from fresh-pressed sugarcane juice, not molasses. Fermentation often runs wild: spontaneous or driven by native yeasts, and the liquid gets distilled just once to preserve its raw, grassy soul.

Styles split two ways: Prata (unaged) stays bright, vegetal, cocktail-ready. Amarela (aged) rests in native Brazilian woods like amburana, balsam, or jequitibá, each leaving its tropical fingerprint. Industrial cachaça gets mass-produced in column stills. The real stuff stays artisanal, pot-distilled in copper by hands that follow rhythm, not recipes.

Bottle to Bar

Cachaça cuts through citrus like a blade. It's the backbone of the Caipirinha, Brazil's national cocktail: lime, sugar, and spirit, crushed and shaken like a street drum. But aged cachaça belongs in a snifter, where its spice and wood can stretch out. Expect notes of green banana, raw sugar, cinnamon, or forest floor, depending on the barrel and the hand that filled it. It's not smooth. It's not soft. It's real.

Furidian's Field Notes

Cachaça is rum's wild cousin: unpolished, unapologetic, and proud of it. It was once so popular it threatened Portuguese wine imports, so the crown banned it in 1635. The ban lasted nearly 200 years and turned every cachaça drinker into a quiet rebel. Today, Brazil produces 1.3 billion liters annually but exports less than 1%; they keep the good stuff for themselves.

The word "cachaça" comes from "cachaza," Spanish for "worthless." The Brazilians took the insult and made it a badge of honor. Real cachaça ages in woods that don't exist anywhere else on earth: trees like amburana that give it notes of cinnamon and vanilla that French oak never could. Haiti's clairin and the French Caribbean's rhum agricole share the same cane juice soul, each shouting in its own regional dialect.

Cachaça

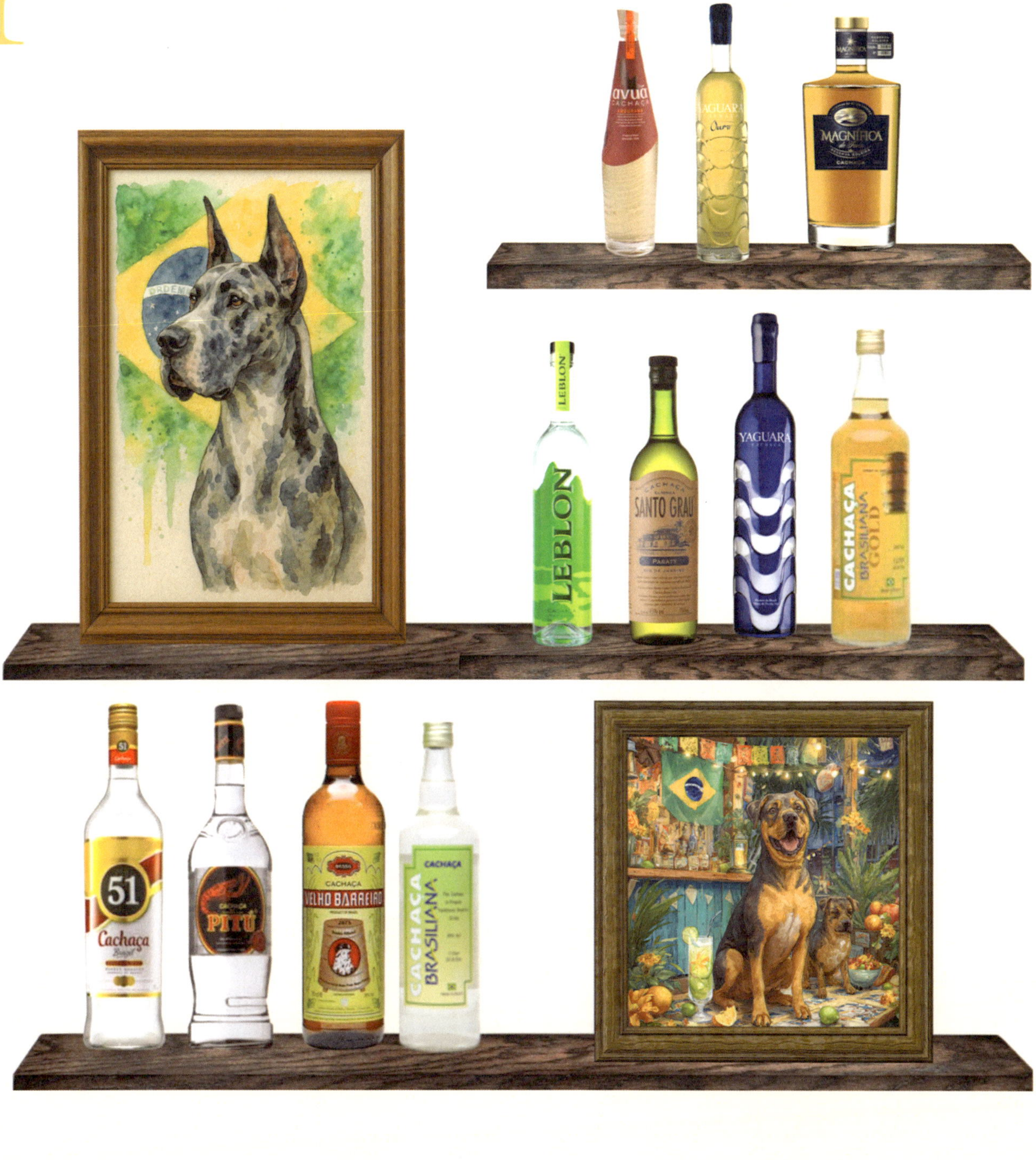
avuá
CACHAÇA
YAGUARA
Ouro
MAGNÍFICA
CACHAÇA
ORDEM
LEBLON
LEBLON
CACHAÇA
SANTO GRAU
PARATY
YAGUARA
CACHAÇA
BRASILIANA
GOLD
51
Cachaça
PITU
CACHAÇA
VELHO BARREIRO
CACHAÇA
CACHAÇA
BRASILIANA

Cachaça

Brand	Style	Notes
Cachaça 51	Industrial	Clean, peppery, widely used in Brazilian bars
Pitu	Industrial	Punchy, dry, classic Caipirinha base
Velho Barreiro	Industrial	Light, floral, super affordable
Brasiliana Silver	Artisanal (Unaged)	Mild, clean, vegetal, ideal for Caipirinhas

Brand	Style	Notes
Leblon	Light-aged	French oak-aged, vanilla tones, smooth and soft
Santo Grau Paraty	Artisanal	Fermented in stone vats, earthy and terroir-rich
Yaguara Blue	Blended Artisanal	Bright, balanced, ideal for elevated cocktails
Brasiliana Gold	Oak-aged Artisanal	Balanced spice, light vanilla and toast

Brand	Style	Notes
Cachaça 51	Industrial	Clean, peppery, widely used in Brazilian bars
Pitu	Industrial	Punchy, dry, classic Caipirinha base
Velho Barreiro	Industrial	Light, floral, super affordable
Brasiliana Silver	Artisanal (Unaged)	Mild, clean, vegetal, ideal for Caipirinhas

Absinthe

Roots and Rumors
Born in Swiss apothecaries and raised in bohemian Parisian cafés, absinthe is an ancient herbal tonic wrapped in scandal. Nicknamed "The Green Fairy," it became the muse of artists and the nemesis of moral authorities. By the early 1900s, it was banned across Europe and the U.S., blamed for everything from madness to moral collapse, sometimes all three at once. But behind the hysteria lived a spirit with deep herbal roots and a mystique that still haunts every proper bar. The fairy never really disappeared; she just learned to wait.

Map and Method
Absinthe begins with high-proof neutral spirit, infused with botanicals, especially grande wormwood, green anise, and sweet fennel. Then it is often redistilled to concentrate the herbal essence. Bottled between 45-74% ABV, it's built for transformation, not sipping. What sets absinthe apart is the louche: when cold water slowly drips over a sugar cube into the glass, essential oils emulsify, turning the clear spirit into cloudy jade or milky opal. This isn't theater; it's chemistry. The cloudier it gets, the better the botanical concentration. Real absinthe contains no added sugar after distillation. It's not a liqueur. It's an herbal spirit that demands respect.

Bottle to Bar
Absinthe rewards restraint. Used sparingly in cocktails due to its high proof and bold anise profile, a little commandeers the entire drink. Think of it as the ghost in your cocktail: invisible until it isn't. Three ways to harness the fairy: Rinse (coat the glass, dump the excess: pure aromatics), Dash or Drop (a few drops as a modifier transform everything), or The Ritual (traditional service with slotted spoon, sugar cube, and ice water at 3:1 to 5:1 dilution).

Furidian's Field Notes
Absinthe teaches patience in an impatient world. It doesn't mix well with impulse or ego. The louche, that signature clouding when water meets spirit, is chemistry, not special effects. Real absinthe turns opalescent naturally; it doesn't need dyes, gimmicks, or neon green. The ritual exists for good reason: cold water activates the botanicals, sugar balances the bitter wormwood, and the slow pour prevents shocking the oils. It's not a ceremony; it's a function. Rush it, and you've wasted something special. The real test: If the label doesn't list wormwood or Artemisia absinthium, it isn't absinthe: it's marketing with an accent. Find a bottle that lists its botanicals like a pharmacy inventory, then treat it like the liquid history it is. The Green Fairy doesn't perform tricks. She reveals truths, if you're patient enough to listen.

 # Brandy

Roots and Rumors
Brandy is what happens when wine grows up. The name comes from the Dutch *brandewijn*, "burnt wine," a nod to its origins as a preservation method for wine that evolved into something far more sophisticated. Made from fermented fruit juice (grapes, apples, pears, cherries), it once graced the tables of kings and clergy alike. Over centuries, it migrated from palaces to punch bowls, from cathedrals to cigar lounges. Wherever refinement met fire, brandy followed.

Map and Method
At its essence, brandy is fermented fruit juice, distilled and aged in oak. Most brandies come from grapes, but regional varieties use apples (Calvados), cherries (Kirsch), pears, or even apricots. Aging in oak brings warm notes of vanilla, spice, and dried fruit. It's not just tradition; it's transformation. Brandy gains depth with time. The distillation method matters. Pot stills create character and texture. Column stills deliver refinement and clarity. Age classifications tell the story: VS (2+ years) brings bright fruit, VSOP (4+ years) adds depth, XO (10+ years) delivers full complexity. Time isn't just aging; it's alchemy.

Bottle to Bar
Brandy's natural richness makes it a gracious companion: elegant and neat in a snifter, confident in cocktails. Classics like the Sidecar, Brandy Alexander, and Vieux Carré rely on its round, mellow backbone to anchor the drink without dominating. When mixing, treat brandy like a seasoned dinner guest: give it respect, then let it do the talking. It brings warmth without overwhelming, sweetness without cloying. Skip unnecessary sugar or aggressive citrus; brandy doesn't need help holding the room.

Furidian's Field Notes
In the 1700s, American doctors prescribed brandy for everything from fevers to fainting spells. George Washington included it in daily Revolutionary War rations. The medical claims were nonsense, but the comfort remains real. Brandy still carries that old-world reputation for warmth and recovery. In hot toddies, it offers a smooth, fruit-forward alternative to whiskey, pairing effortlessly with honey, lemon, and warming spices. A colonial cure? No. A timeless comfort? Absolutely. Sometimes the best medicine is simply knowing when to pour a proper drink.

Brandy

Brandy is the slow conversation at the end of a long evening, the final word in a glass.
~ Furidian

Brandy

Brand	Age	Region	Flavor Profile
Germain-Robin XO	XO	USA (California)	Floral, grape-forward, refined, Pinot Noir
Fundador Supremo 18	18 years	Spain (Jerez)	Oloroso sherry notes, toffee, oak
Torres 20	20-year solera system	Spain (Catalonia)	Cocoa, cinnamon, dried fruit, smooth
Lepanto Solera Gran Reserva	Solera Gran Reserva	Spain (Jerez)	Elegant, sherry-kissed, dried fruit
Copper & Kings	VS / Reserve	USA (Kentucky)	Bold, fruit-forward, dry, high proof

Brand	Age	Region	Flavor Profile
Carlos I	Solera Gran Reserva	Spain (Jerez)	Spicy oak, vanilla, nutty
Gran Duque d'Alba	Solera Gran Reserva	Spain (Jerez)	Rich, velvety, caramel, raisins
Bardinet VSOP	VSOP	France	Smooth, toasted wood, dried fruit
St-Rémy XO	XO	France	Fig, vanilla, baking spice
Napoleon Brandy	VSOP equivalent	France/Spain	Rich dried fruits, mild spice

Brand	Age	Region	Flavor Profile
Three Barrels	VS / VSOP available	France	Round, soft fruit, vanilla
Korbel	VSOP	USA (California)	Bright, apple, soft spice
Fundador	Solera-aged (non-VSOP)	Spain (Jerez)	Nutty, oaky, soft sherry finish
President	Not specified (young)	USA	Fruity, simple, easy-drinking
E&J	VS / VSOP available	USA	Sweet, smooth, light oak, vanilla

 *Cognac*

Roots and Rumors

Cognac is brandy with standards. Born from trade necessity in the Charente region, what started as a way to preserve wine for export became France's most regulated spirit. AOC laws dictate everything: region, grapes (mostly Ugni Blanc), and double distillation in copper pot stills. What began as a regional trade spirit became a global symbol of refinement. Pressure creates diamonds. Rules create Cognac.

Map and Method

Cognac production is tightly controlled. Grapes are fermented into wine, then distilled twice using traditional copper alembic stills before aging in French oak for a minimum of two years. Most houses go far beyond that, releasing VS (Very Special), VSOP (Very Superior Old Pale), and XO (Extra Old) expressions. The oak adds vanilla, spice, and structure. The aging demands patience and rewards complexity. Every step, from vine to barrel, is traceable, tested, and enforced. No shortcuts allowed.

Bottle to Bar

Cognac is most often sipped neat, but its structure makes it highly mixable if you choose the right bottle. VS and VSOP are built for mixing: bright, fruity, structured enough for Sidecars and French 75s without breaking the bank. XO is for contemplation, not cocktails. Serve neat, slightly warmed, in a proper snifter. Store bottles upright. And remember: Cognac doesn't need ice, mixers, or apologies. It earned its reputation the hard way.

Furidian's Field Notes

Every Cognac is brandy, but not every brandy earns the name Cognac. France drew the borders in 1909 and codified the rules in 1936. Since then, Cognac has been the standard for what disciplined distillation and patient aging should taste like. The label means something: it passed the test. In a world full of marketing and shortcuts, Cognac still plays by the old rules. Respect that.

Cognac

Cognac

Brand	Age	Region	Flavor Profile
Camus Borderies XO	XO	Cognac, FR	Floral, violet, honey, dried apricot
Rémy Martin XO	XO	Cognac, FR	Fig, cinnamon, mature oak
Hennessy XO	XO	Cognac, FR	Dark chocolate, spice, candied fruit
D'Ussé XO	XO	Cognac, FR	Almond, stewed fruit, leather
Hennessy Paradis	Paradis (blend)	Cognac, FR	Jasmine, truffle, cardamom, dried rose
Louis XIII	Blend (100+ yrs)	Cognac, FR	Nutmeg, sandalwood, fig, tobacco, leather

Brand	Age	Region	Flavor Profile
Hennessy VSOP	VSOP	Cognac, France	Balanced, oak, vanilla, spice
Rémy Martin 1738	VSOP+	Cognac, France	Toasted oak, fig, butterscotch, dried fruit
Courvoisier XO	XO	Cognac, France	Candied orange, crème brûlée, iris
A.E. Dor XO	XO	Cognac, France	Elegant spice, dried flowers, woodsy leather
Louis Royer XO	XO	Cognac, France	Praline, tobacco, spice-rich with silky depth
Martell Cordon Bleu	XO+	Cognac, France	Elegant and round, fruitcake, spice, long finish

Brand	Age	Region	Flavor Profile
Martell VS	VS	Cognac, FR	Light fruit, oak, crisp finish
Courvoisier VS	VS	Cognac, FR	Apple, pear, floral
Rémy Martin VSOP	VSOP	Cognac, FR	Stone fruit, vanilla, baking spice
Hennessy VS	VS	Cognac, FR	Toast, almond, green grape
Camus VSOP	VSOP	Cognac, FR	Citrus peel, pepper, plum
Hardy VSOP	VSOP	Cognac, FR	Nutty, smooth, fig
Pierre Ferrand 1840	3-Star/VS	Cognac, FR	Baked apple, floral, spice

Armagnac

Roots and Rumors
Armagnac is France's oldest distilled spirit, born in the Gascon countryside nearly 700 years ago, centuries before its more famous cousins. While Cognac courted kings, Armagnac stayed home in family distilleries, quietly perfecting its craft for generations. No marketing budgets. No celebrity endorsements. Only tradition and the patience passed down through generations of Gascon distillers.

Map and Method
Armagnac uses single distillation through a copper alambic armagnacais, a continuous still that distills once instead of Cognac's two-pass method. Four main grapes create the blend: Baco, Folle Blanche, Colombard, and Ugni Blanc. Local black oak does the aging work, developing notes of prune, tobacco, vanilla, and spice over years of patient maturation. Single distillation prioritizes character over efficiency, resulting in deeper, more textured flavors.

Bottle to Bar
Where Cognac smooths edges, Armagnac keeps them sharp. Single distillation preserves rough charm that makes it an anchor for bold cocktails: a Sazerac with farmhouse grit instead of parlor polish. VS and VSOP expressions bring enough character to hold stirred drinks together without emptying your wallet. Vintage Armagnac offers something rare. Most spirits blend years together for consistency, but Armagnac producers regularly release single-harvest bottlings that capture specific seasons. A 1985 Armagnac holds the weather, soil conditions, and character of that exact year. These bottles offer complexity shaped by time and place, not blending formulas.

Furidian's Field Notes
In 2010, Armagnac became the first French spirit granted Protected Geographical Indication (PGI) status by the European Union: a quiet badge of honor for a brandy that's never begged for applause. It's still made in small, family-run distilleries, often by Gascon locals who've been at it for generations. Ask an Armagnac maker who they distill for, and the answer's simple: "Those who know." While Cognac courts the crowd, Armagnac keeps handwritten records and lets centuries of flavor do the talking. It's France's best-kept secret, hiding in plain sight.

# Armagnac

Armagnac

Brand/Label	Age	Region	Flavor Profile
Delord 20 Ans d'Âge (Round)	20 Years	Bas-Armagnac	Rich, prune, walnut, leather, rancio
Castarède XO 20 Ans d'Âge	20 Years	Bas-Armagnac	Vanilla, oak, dried fruits, caramel
Delord 25 Ans (Tall Bottle)	25 Years	Bas-Armagnac	Butterscotch, almond, dark chocolate
Darroze Les Grands Assemblages 20	20 Years	Bas-Armagnac	Elegant, dried fruit, cigar box, finesse
Château de Laubade 1989	Vintage 1989	Bas-Armagnac	Dried fig, tobacco, roasted nuts, spice
Castarède 1985	Vintage 1985	Bas-Armagnac	Spicy wood, raisin, dry fruit, floral notes
Laberdolive 1992	Vintage 1992	Bas-Armagnac	Elegant, herbal, citrus peel, silky oak

Brand/Label	Age	Region	Flavor Profile
Armagnac de Montal XO	XO (~10 yrs)	Bas-Armagnac	Smooth, vanilla, prune, light spice
Clos Martin XO 15	15 Years	Bas-Armagnac	Toffee, roasted nuts, subtle rancio, dried fruit
Dartigalongue XO	XO (~10 yrs)	Bas-Armagnac	Honeyed, nutty, round texture, warming finish
Marie Duffau Hors d'Âge	~12–15 Years	Bas-Armagnac	Spiced wood, floral notes, dried apricot, soft oak
Château de Laubade XO	XO (~12 yrs)	Bas-Armagnac	Candied citrus, cocoa, nutmeg, elegant tannin
Domaine de Baraillon 1992	Vintage 1992	Bas-Armagnac	Earthy, old oak, tobacco, cooked plum

Brand/Label	Age	Region	Flavor Profile
Clés des Ducs VSOP	VSOP (~4–6 yrs)	Bas-Armagnac	Raisin, caramel, baked apple
Samalens VSOP	VSOP (~4–6 yrs)	Bas-Armagnac	Soft vanilla, dried apricot, toasted oak
Saint-Vivant VSOP	VSOP (~4–6 yrs)	Armagnac	Dried fruit, baking spice, touch of oak
Waitrose Armagnac VSOP	VSOP (~4–6 yrs)	Bas-Armagnac	Mellow fruit, spice, simple oak
Armin 6	6 Years	Bas-Armagnac	Bright, fresh fruit, spice, light oak
Marquis de Montesquiou VSOP	VSOP (~4–6 yrs)	Armagnac	Smooth, apricot, vanilla, mild spice
Janneau VSOP Grand Armagnac	VSOP (4–7 yrs)	Ténarèze	Honey, white pepper, almond

Navy Strength

In the 18th century, the British Royal Navy issued daily rations of rum and gin to sailors. But on a ship full of gunpowder and cannon fire, proof of potency mattered, literally. If a barrel leaked onto the gunpowder, and the powder still ignited, the spirit was deemed strong enough to serve aboard. That benchmark? 57% alcohol by volume, or 114 proof.

Thus was born the term "Navy Strength" not a marketing flourish, but a historical standard born of necessity, precision, and maritime grit.

While modern spirits typically bottle at 40–45% ABV, Navy Strength versions preserve that higher proof, delivering more flavor, structure, and heat. They're favored in classic cocktails where dilution is expected like martinis, tonics, or shaken drinks, ensuring the spirit holds its shape.

Spirit	Retail ABV/Proof	Navy ABV/Proof
Gin	40%/80	57%/114
Rum	40%/80	57-75%/114-151
Whiskey	40%/80	50–57%/100–114
Vodka	40%/80	50–57%/100–114
Tequila	40%/80	50–55%/100–110
Mezcal	45%/90	50–58%/100–116
Absinthe	45-60%/90-120	60–74%/120–148
Everclear	60%/120	75–95%/151-190

Liqueurs & Cordials: The Finishing Touch
The pour that dresses the drink. A little goes a long way.

Roots and Rumors
Liqueurs (sometimes called cordials) are the flamboyant eccentrics of the spirits world, infused with flavor, softened with sugar. They began in apothecaries and monasteries, originally crafted as medicinal tonics. Over time, they sweet-talked their way into courts, cafés, and cocktail menus across the globe. Today, the terms are interchangeable, but the purpose remains the same: bold, expressive, and indulgent. From orange-kissed triple sec to velvety creams and peanut butter novelties, liqueurs transform ordinary drinks into liquid desserts or add the perfect finishing touch to a classic cocktail. They're not about subtlety; they're about making every sip memorable.

Map and Method
Liqueurs start with a base spirit: vodka, rum, brandy, or whiskey, then absorb flavor from fruits, nuts, herbs, spices, or creams. By law, they must contain at least 2.5% sugar by volume, which explains their signature sweetness. Most settle between 15-30% ABV, though some pack a stronger punch. The categories tell the story of global tastes: fruit-based liqueurs like Cointreau and Chambord bring brightness; nut and bean varieties like amaretto and coffee liqueurs add richness; herbal powerhouses like Jägermeister and Chartreuse deliver complexity; cream-based spirits like Irish cream offer indulgence. Then there are the novelties: peanut butter, birthday cake, cinnamon. Proof that someone, somewhere, will turn any flavor into a bottle.

Bottle to Bar
Liqueurs are the sweet-talking charmers of the back bar. They are accents used to elevate, not to overpower. They bring sweetness, texture, and character, but their richness comes with responsibility. Behind any respectable bar, one golden rule applies: Never use more than ½ ounce of a sugary liqueur when mixing with other sweet elements. Let the liqueur sing, not scream. A good cocktail is like music: the spirit leads, the liqueur harmonizes, and sugar doesn't steal the solo.

Furidian's Field Notes
In 1930s France, Cointreau marketed itself as "the perfect liqueur for women": light, sweet, and elegant. The marketing conveniently omitted that it was 80 proof and typically served neat. Turns out "light, sweet, and elegant" doesn't mean weak; it means dangerously smooth. These weren't party tricks or novelty flavors. They were centuries of botanical knowledge, distilled into bottles. The monks understood something essential: the right combination of herbs, spirits, and patience could create something that tasted like liquid alchemy. That tradition lives on in every properly made liqueur, even the ones that taste like birthday cake.

Liquor ~ Nut, Chocolate, Coffee

Almond Hazelnut Macadamia Walnut Peanut Butter

Chocolate and Chocolate Blends

Coffee & Coffee/Cream   Horchata/Cinnamon

Liquor ~ Herbal & Botanical Liqueurs

Licorice/Anise   Elderflower   Violet

Mint   Peppermint   Cinnamon   Bitters

> "It's not just the base that builds the drink, it's the finish that makes it memorable."
> ~Furidian

Herbal Elixirs & Monastic Roots

Non-Alcoholic Spirits
All of the tradition. All of the ritual. None of the alcohol.

Syrup Flavor Guide

 ### Fruity & Refreshing Flavors
Best in: Fruit Teas, Lemonades, Smoothies
Raspberry – Zingy and bright
Peach – Juicy and sweet
Strawberry – Sweet and refreshing
Blueberry – Sweet with tart balance
Mango – Tropical and vibrant
Green Apple – Crisp and tart
Watermelon – Sweet and light
Lavender – Floral

 ### Classic & Creamy Flavors
Best in: Coffee, Frappes, Milk Teas
Vanilla – Sweet and creamy
Caramel – Rich, buttery
Hazelnut – Nutty and smooth
Chocolate – Velvety and indulgent
Almond – Subtle nutty depth
Irish Cream – Whiskey-cream flavored
Toffee – Buttery sweetness

 ### Tropical & Exotic Flavors
Best in: Smoothies, Frappes, Tropical Fruit Teas
Coconut – Creamy, exotic profile
Pina Colada – Pineapple + coconut

 ### Seasonal & Spiced Flavors
Best in: Coffee, Frappes, Chai, Winter Drinks
Cinnamon – Warm and spicy
Gingerbread – Spiced
Mint – Cool and refreshing; great for hot chocolate and festive coffees

Legal Disclaimer

The information, recipes, and content in Furidian's Pawtender's Pour are intended for educational, entertainment, and lifestyle purposes only. This book does not provide veterinary advice, medical guidance, or nutritional treatment for animals or humans.

All pet-friendly recipes were developed with care and informed by general safety standards from reputable sources, including the ASPCA, AKC, and the Pet Poison Helpline. However, every animal is different. Sensitivities, allergies, and underlying health conditions vary widely. Always consult a licensed veterinarian before introducing new foods, treats, or beverages into your pet's routine. The authors, contributors, and publisher disclaim any liability for adverse reactions, injuries, or health conditions that may result from the use or misuse of the information provided. All ingredients and recommendations are offered in good faith but are not guaranteed to be appropriate for every animal.

All cocktail recipes in this book include alcohol suggestions and are intended for responsible adult consumption. Please drink responsibly. Never serve alcohol to minors or animals.
All brand names, product references, and trademarks mentioned throughout the book are the property of their respective owners. Their inclusion is for informational and educational purposes only and does not imply endorsement or affiliation with Furidian's Pawtender's Pour or Furidian Lifestyle™.

By using this book, you accept full responsibility for how you apply, adapt, or interpret its content. When in doubt, consult a qualified professional.

Portions of this book may have been created or enhanced using AI tools and were curated by the authors to ensure clarity, accuracy, and intent.

© 2025 Furidian Lifestyle™. All rights reserved.
Furidian Lifestyle™ is a trademark of Furidian Lifestyle LLC.
No part of this publication may be reproduced or distributed in any form without prior written permission, except for brief excerpts used in reviews or educational settings.

This book is dedicated to the best man ever, Blake.
He found me in a place forgotten, bruised, broken, and thrown away.
But he didn't just lift me from a dumpster. He lifted my soul.

We are not man and mutt. We are brothers. Bound not by blood, but by every meal shared, every mile driven, every moment we stood side by side.

We've traveled the country together and when "On the Road Again" played, I didn't hesitate. I leapt into the truck, tail high, heart full, ready for whatever came next, because wherever we were headed, it was together.

He fed me steak, chicken, and love. He gave me a home, a purpose, and the kind of loyalty of which most people only dream.
I wasn't rescued. I was chosen. And I chose him right back.

With a full belly and fuller heart,
  ~Furidian

To Brigitte, Luke, Helena, Avalon, and especially Grandma and Grandad.
Thank you for letting me visit, overstay, shed everywhere, bark too loud, and still call your place home. I know I wasn't always easy. You flinched when I jumped on people, on couches, and occasionally on countertops. You braced yourselves as I dragged you across sidewalks, left fur on every surface, slobbered on sleeves, and made myself known in every room. You cringed when I stole the pillow pet. You forgave muddy pawprints on clean floors. You never stayed mad when I flooded the bathroom after a shower.

But the truth is, I loved hard. I loved with my tail, with my bark, and with my whole goofy heart.
And what I'll remember most is how we always found our way back to each other. Even after months apart, I ran to you like no time had passed. Because your scent, your voice, your hugs, your smile, they weren't just familiar. That's home. That's family.

I was never just a pet in your house. I was your shadow with a heartbeat.
Your chaos with a collar. Your tornado with a tail.
Your other son, brother, and granddog.
With loyalty louder than my bark,
  ~Furidian

Furidian Lifestyle

Furidian Friends
Pours with Pourpose

Rescue. Rebuild. Rehome.

A portion of every purchase supports Furidian Friends is our nonprofit dedicated to rescuing, rehabilitating, and rehoming pets, turning discarded lives into legacies.

Every pour honors the dog still waiting for a home.

Coastal Designs

Planners & Journals

Furidian Pawntender Bartending & Mixology

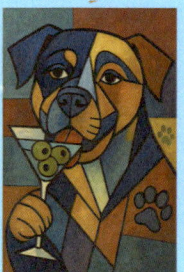

AI Pet Personalization: Images, Artwork, and Videos

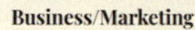
FuridianLifestyle.com

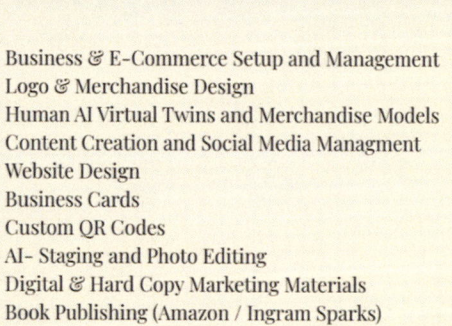

Business/Marketing

- Business & E-Commerce Setup and Management
- Logo & Merchandise Design
- Human AI Virtual Twins and Merchandise Models
- Content Creation and Social Media Managment
- Website Design
- Business Cards
- Custom QR Codes
- AI- Staging and Photo Editing
- Digital & Hard Copy Marketing Materials
- Book Publishing (Amazon / Ingram Sparks)
- Chatbot and Automation

www.ingramcontent.com/pod-product-compliance
Lightning Source LLC
Chambersburg PA
CBRC091204010526
44107CB00021B/1245